LOOKING AHEAD:

Self-conceptions, Race and Family as Determinants of Adolescent Orientation to Achievement

by

Chad Gordon

Published for the Arnold M. and Caroline Rose Monograph Series, American Sociological Association.

THE ARNOLD AND CAROLINE ROSE MONOGRAPH SERIES IN SOCIOLOGY

A gift by Arnold and Caroline Rose to the American Sociological Association in 1968 provided for the establishment of the Arnold and Caroline Rose Monograph Series in Sociology. The conveyance provided for the publication of manuscripts in any subject matter field of sociology. The donors intended the series for rather short monographs, contributions that normally are beyond the scope of publication in regular academic journals.

The Series is under the general direction of an editorial board appointed by the Council of the American Sociological Association and responsible to the Publications Committee of the Association. Competition for publication in the Series has been limited by the Association to Fellow, Active and Student members.

THE ARNOLD AND CAROLINE ROSE MONOGRAPH SERIES IN ECOLOGY

Library of Congress Number 77-183121
International Standard Book Number 0-912764-02-3

1722 N St. N.W.
Washington, D.C. 20036

TABLE OF CONTENTS

I

I. ORIENTATION

Young, urban black youths' self-hatred and feelings of incompetent dependence and their angry alienation from social institutions are commonly held to result from their life experiences and to prevent them from taking advantage of available opportunities. In a burgeoning literature on the subject of the attitudes of black youth four sets of presumed causal factors in their life experiences have received greatest attention:

First, the cultural residues of slavery and the "Sambo" stereotype have been delineated, historically by Elkins (1963) and contemporaneously by Silberman (1964) and Pettigrew (1964, 1965).

Second, factors of the social structure, in all the senses in which Weber speaks of structure, have made up a large measure of the discussion: economic class (e.g., Dollard, 1937, especially ch. 5-8, 17; Drake, 1965) and status or caste (Dollard, 1937, especially ch. 9-16, 18; Davis, Gardner and Gardner, 1941; Drake and Cayton, 1945; Warner and Srole, 1945; Frazier, 1957; and Clark, 1965) have predominated. Power or political aspects of the life situation of black regained the attention of social scientists with the rise of the Civil Rights Movement in the 1950's and its replacement by the Black Power Movement in the 1960's (cf. Clark, 1966; Carmichael and Hamilton, 1967; Barbour, 1968; and Killian, 1968).

The third major area of research and theory concerns the direct social-psychological effects of immediate racial prejudice and discrimination (Stonequist, 1937; Davis and Dollard, 1940; Clark and Clark, 1947; Kardiner and Ovesey, 1951; Goodman 1952; Rohrer and Edmonson, 1960). Traumatic crises throughout the life cycle (Coles, 1964; Erikson, 1966; Grier and Cobbs, 1968), and vivid autobiographies and sensitive observational studies have made important contributions (Wright, 1937; Haley and Malcolm X, 1964; Brown, 1965; Liebow, 1966; Kozol, 1967; David, 1968). Long steps toward formulating and pulling together the theoretical generalizations emerging from the work in culture, macro-social structures and psychological development have been taken by Simpson and Yinger (1965), Blalock (1967), and the authors contributing to the Deutsch (1968) collection.

Fourth, intertwined with research in race relations is a long-standing and sometimes confused concern with the impact of the immediate family on the lives of black children in terms of its structure, socialization and interaction patterns. To a large extent, this concern arises in the conjuncture of previous work on the presumed effects of the father's absence on children of whatever race with the more recent sharply focused studies of economic, social and cultural factors making black families especially prone to disruption through death, divorce or separation. Discussions of severe difficulties faced by black families have been on hand for many years, especially in the work of E. Franklin Frazier (1937, 1939, 1957), Davis and Dollard (1940), and Davis, Gardner and Gardner (1941). Yet it took the politically dramatic "Moynihan Report" *(The Negro Family: The Case for National Action,* by Daniel Patrick Moynihan, 1965, issued with some secrecy by the U.S. Department of Labor) and the ensuing acrimonious and exceptionally ideological controversy to rivet attention on the ways in which the black family is implicated in a cycle of poverty and a "tangle of pathology." In *The Moynihan Report and the Politics of Controversy,* Lee Rainwater and William L. Yancey (1967) served a valuable function, making widely available the original government report and a large number of relevant evaluations by members of the "permanent government," civil rights leaders, political journalists, and interested academics, together with a detailed chronicle of the shifting pressures and antagonisms surrounding release of the document and an analysis of its potential impact on policy or legislation. However, the vast bulk of the critical discussion contained in the Rainwater and Yancey volume was an assessment of the effects of slavery, poverty, and unemployment in producing five generally agreed-upon outcomes documented in various government statistical compilations:

1) As of the time of the 1960 Census, about 23% of ever-married non-white females in urban areas were separated, divorced or otherwise estranged from their husbands, as compared to approximately 8% of white females;

2) About 23% of all non-white families were headed by females (as compared to some 90% of white families);

3) At least 24% of non-white births were out of wedlock, as against about 3% of white births;

4) Less than 50% of non-white children reach the age of 18, having lived all their lives with both parents, (no comparative data were given for whites);

5) Approximately 56% of non-white children would at some time be recipients of public assistance, compared to 8% of white children (Moynihan, 1965: 52-55).

Moynihan further asserted that all of these forms of what was called "family instability" among blacks were increasing at a rate far in excess of comparable change among whites:

> But there is one truly great discontinuity in family structure in the present time: that between the world of white American in general and that of the Negro American.
>
> The white family has achieved a high degree of stability and is maintaining that stability.
>
> *By contrast, the family structure of lower-class Negroes is highly unstable, and in many urban centers is approaching complete breakdown.* (*ibid.*, p. 51, emphasis in original)

Although Moynihan elsewhere indicates that unemployment probably has the same effect on blacks as on whites (*ibid.*, p. 65), he did not draw upon the Census for data to compare blacks and whites of the same social class. Thus the unrestricted generalizations and the major thrust of the Report presented family disruption as primarily a "Negro problem," largely the heritage of slavery. Many analysts have feared that the Report might thus be used as the basis of governmental programs aimed directly at black families instead of at the more fundamental problems of unemployment and underemployment that afflict poverty-stricken whites as well. (e.g., Herzog, 1966:346-350; Sheppard and Stringer, 1966).

In the midst of all the discussion of what might have produced particular configurations of family structure among low-income blacks (or whites), the essential link between family structure and "pathology" was generally assumed. This monograph is an attempt to provide some of the lacking theoretical structure and to evaluate more of the necessary empirical evidence of this logically necessary but previously implicit connecting link between large-scale institutional factors and individual socialization.*

The "tangle of pathology" described by Pettigrew (1964), Clark (1965) and Moynihan (1965:76-91) is hypothesized to originate in matriarchal

* I would like to express my appreciation to James Coleman, Daniel Patrick Moynihan, Thomas Pettigrew and David Armor for making data available to me and to my students. I am very grateful also to Mrs. Robin Chard for her exceptionally skilled research assistance and aid in preparation of the manuscript, to Miss Anne Kessler for her careful handling of the typing, to Mrs. Betty Clinton for final manuscript preparation and to the graphics staff of the Southwest Center for Urban Research for preparation of the rather complex figures. Special thanks are due to Otis Dudley Duncan for his thorough and pungent criticism of the draft. Many of his suggestions concerning the path analysis and other aspects of the presentation have been incorporated here; I alone am responsible for any errors. Finally, my special thanks go to Helen MacGill Hughes for her extremely thorough and helpful editing.

dominance over a fatherless home or a home in which the male plays an economically weak role, the effect of which is to create severe difficulties for the children, especially the sons. Among the asserted outcomes of father's absence are inability to delay gratification, perception of the world as hostile, poor performance in school and on tests of mental ability, low educational aspiration, high rates of juvenile delinquency and violent crime, high rates of rejection by the armed forces, and withdrawal from society by way of addiction to alcohol or narcotics.

Most damaging of all is the young black boy's probable difficulty in developing a clear, strong, and positive conceptions of self, especially regarding his masculinity (Pettigrew, 1964:15-26; Rainwater, 1966). In this cycle of poverty and pain—so runs the argument—black males in particular are thus unable to fulfill their "normal" sex roles and will despair of possible ahievement and upward occupational mobility (Whiting and Burton, 1961; Liebow, 1966). Naturally, the consequent lowered aspiration and reduced effort will make the prophecy of probable failure come true (Kardiner and Ovesey, 1951; Rosenthal and Jacobson, 1968). Relevant to this thesis is the question of the existence and pervasiveness of a general culture of poverty (e.g., Lewis, 1965; Ferman, *et al.,* 1965, Part 5, including diverse papers by Miller; Rodman, Riessman, and Seagull; and Gans; also see Podell, 1969, for data on New York City welfare families).

Sociologists reason that in general the culture of poverty produces disrupted families and the asserted outcomes among socially and economically marginal groups of whatever race. This is in direct contrast to the historic and specific argument that slavery and its consequences produced a special set of "Negro problems." In order to test and evaluate the more general model, it is necessary to construct a set of logically connected hypotheses concerning the relationships among race, the family's role structure, aspects of self-conception, and children's aspirations. Avoiding some of the logical difficulties of the Moynihan controversies, an adequate test of the hypotheses is a comparison of these relationships in which social class is taken into account, since a very substantial body of research has demonstrated the impact of social class on life aspiration. Important instances are Hollingshead (1949); Empey (1956); Sewell, Haller, and Strauss (1957); Stephenson (1957); Elder (1962b), Turner (1964); most of the studies summarized in Goldstein (1967, ch. 2-3); the exceptionally comprehensive research of Blau and Duncan (1967); Duncan, Haller, and Portes (1968); Duncan and Duncan (1969).

In addition, such an investigation should take account of three further complexities generally glossed over or ignored completely in previous analyses. First, while numerous theorists and practitioners have discussed the importance of self-conception in mediating past socialization and future conduct (see the extensive and diverse writings collected in Gordon and Gergen, 1968), it is rare for relatively specific aspects of self-conception to be delineated and measured in a context of actual empirical research (Wylie, 1961; Gordon, 1968b). Race, class, and family structure are assumed to interact, each in its own way, to shape such dimensions of self-conception as basic self-acceptance, self-perceived mental capacity and academic ability, the sense of general competence and of self-determination, and finally, the global evaluative dimension, self-esteem. In the socio-cognitive theoretical perspective being used here, these are all aspects of self-conception—the structure of meanings referable to the self which are available to the individual (Gordon, 1966, 1968a, 1968b, 1968c).

Second, although the bulk of existing research on the effect of differing family structures has focused on a single father-absent/father-present dichotomy (e.g., Davis and Dollard, 1940; Sears, Pintler and Sears, 1946; Whiting and Burton, 1961; Moynihan, 1965), more recent analyses (Rainwater, 1966; Gordon and Shea, 1967) point to the possibility that a present but weak male role model may be even more damaging to the development of a favorable self-conception than is an absent father.

Third, even when race and social class are taken into account in examining the relationship between family structure and self-conception or aspiration, it must be remembered that these *general* relations will always be mediated by the interaction between particular children with relevant levels of apparent mental ability and particular adults who differ in their aspirations for their differing children. Parental factors and various forms of family experience have been shown to be related to achievement and aspiration in a number of studies (e.g., Dynes, Clark and Dinitz, 1956; Rosen and D'Andrade, 1959; Rosen, 1961; and Sewell and Shah, 1968; Rosen, 1969). Measured intelligence or academic ability has less frequently been included in research on aspiration, but where used it has been found to be strongly related to both educational and occupational aspiration (Gordon, 1963; Eckland, 1965; Sewell and Shah, 1967; Duncan, Haller, and Portes, 1968; Elder, 1968). Therefore both parental influence and measured ability are included in the developing of a comprehensive model.

In the constructing of a theoretical model this orientation involves the simultaneous consideration of the mutual relations between four sets of variables: (1) basic social structural categories (race and social class); (2) immediate social arrangements (family role structure); (3) specific intervening factors (measured mental ability of the child, parental aspiration, and relevant self-conceptions); and, finally, (4) hypothesized behavioral and attitudinal outcomes (educational aspiration, actual school achievement and selection, and occupational expectation).

It should be clear that this simultaneous consideration and the "other-things-being-equal" clause necessitate techniques of analysis and display that are much more subtle and comprehensive than simple zero-order correlation or cross-tabulation, as has been forcefully and clearly argued by Blalock (1964). In this monograph, multiple-control cross-tabulations will be presented first in order to show graphically the nature of the complex relations. Then an attempt will be made to employ the technique, relatively new to sociology, called path analysis, as the procedure most appropriate in discussing and portraying the mutual and simultaneous relations among independent, intervening, and dependent variables.

II

II. MODEL AND CONSTITUENT PROPOSITIONS

Figure 1 presents one possible hypothetical model of the way in which the general sets of factors might by their interrelations determine the major life aspiration of adolescents. In models of this kind, the general flow of time-bound causation is assumed to be from left to right and each arrow represents an asserted asymmetrical causal relation or "path," (Blalock, 1964; Duncan, 1966; and Land, 1969). The total model will provide the basis of subsequent computation and presentation of path coefficients and of assessment of the effect of variables not included in the system. At present it serves to make the constituent relationships explicit.

The structure shown in Figure 1 produces the following propositions, which were written before inspection of the data to be presented in the following sections:

INDEPENDENT OF THE EFFECTS OF OTHER FACTORS:

1. Black students more often have broken families or weak fathers than do white students.
2. Working-class students more often have broken families or weak fathers than do middle-class students.
3. White parents more frequently urge educational achievement and college attendance upon their children than do black parents. (Here

Figure 1—Hypothetical model of some determinants of aspiration among adolescents. Arrows represent asserted asymmetrical causal relationships between the indicated pairs of variables. The numbers correspond to specific hypotheses to be tested.

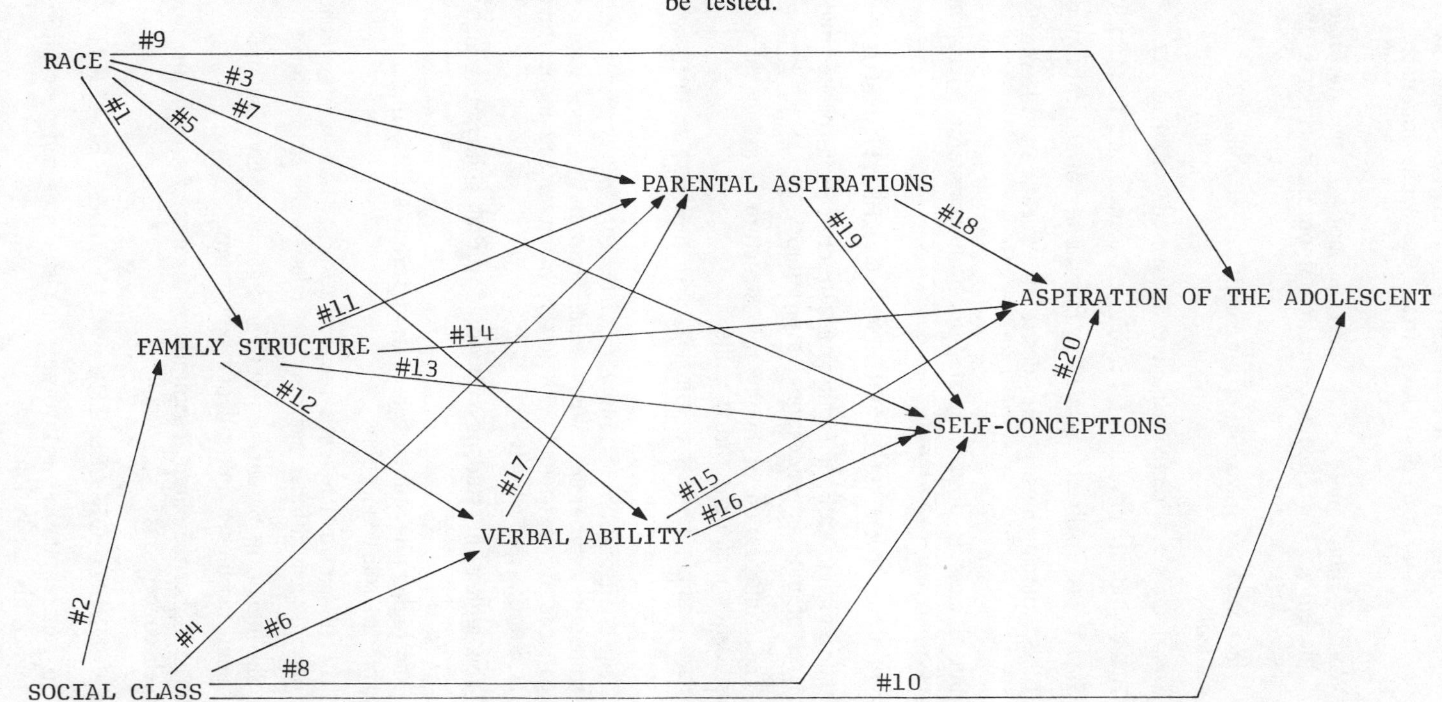

class is important, as it calls into question the general hypothesis of the alienation of blacks from the white-dominated school system.)

4. Working- and middle-class parents more frequently urge high achievement and college education upon their children than do lower-class parents.
5. White students have higher measured verbal ability than do black students.
6. Social class is directly related to measured verbal ability.
7. Black students have less favorable self-conceptions than do whites.
8. Social class is directly related to favorability of self-conceptions.
9. Black students have greater desire for education but lower occupational expectation than do white students.
10. Social class is directly related to both desire for education and occupational expectation.

INDEPENDENT OF THE FOREGOING RELATIONSHIPS:

11. The configuration of family role structure is associated with the level of parents' educational aspiration.
12. The configuration of family role structure is associated with the student's measured verbal ability.
13. The configuration of family role structure is associated with the student's self-conceptions.
14. The configuration of family role structure is associated with the student's aspirations. Weak-male, matriarchy, and strong male patterns are associated with lower, medium, and higher levels of aspiration, respectively.
15. The higher the student's measured verbal ability, the higher his aspirations.
16. The higher the student's measured verbal ability, the more favorable his self-conceptions.
17. The higher the student's measured verbal ability, the higher his parents' aspirations regarding his educational achievement.
18. The higher the parents' aspirations regarding education and achievement, the higher the student's aspirations.
19. The higher the parental aspirations, the more favorable the student's self-conceptions.

INDEPENDENT OF ALL THE PRECEDING RELATIONS:

20. In general, the more favorable the student's self-conceptions, the higher his aspirations.

III

III. METHOD: SAMPLE, OPERATIONALIZATION, AND INDEX CONSTRUCTION

Fortunately, there has been one very large-scale survey in which data were gathered on race, social class, family structure, individual mental ability, parental aspiration, educational and occupational aspirations of the children, and a limited but still meaningful set of dimensions of self-conception: the massive "Coleman Study," reported in *Equality of Educational Opportunity* (Coleman, *et al.*, 1966). This research was commissioned by the U.S. Office of Education under the requirements of the Civil Rights Act of 1964, in an effort to gain valid information

> "concerning the lack of availability of equal educational opportunities for the individuals by reason of race, color, religion, or national origin in public educational institutions at all levels in the United States, its territories and possessions, and the District of Columbia." (p. iii)

Under the direction of James Coleman of Johns Hopkins University, questionnaires (*ibid.,* pp. 575-736) were designed to collect data from a very large sample of public elementary- and secondary-school students, teachers, principals, and district superintendents concerning three major realms of information: 1) the school's racial composition, social characteristics, educational facilities, academic practices, and curriculum offerings; 2) the teachers' education, experience, verbal ability and attitudes; and 3) the students' ethnic and socioeconomic background, family composition, parental aspirations, patterns of activity, aspirations, and some aspects of current self-conceptions. Only the third category of variables will be considered in the present work.

In September and October of 1965, questionnaires appropriate to each given age level were administered to all of the third, sixth, ninth, and twelfth-grade students and half of the first-grade students attending approximately 4,000 schools across the country. (The sample design and procedures, much too elaborate to describe here, are reported in detail, *ibid.,* pp. 550-565.) The essential features are that 1,170 high schools and their feeder elementary schools were selected to yield a sample of 900,000 pupils. These schools were selected after stratification was accomplished according to seven regions of the country, metropolitan/non-metropolitan and proportion non-white, with the county or its equivalent as the primary sampling unit. In order to be sure that there would be sufficient numbers of non-white students for analysis, the sampling plan was set up to yield 50% non-whites. Thus, simple distributions should not be taken directly as representative of the nation, but this causes no problem since almost all of the tables in the Coleman Report are percentaged separately by race, and usually also by region and metropolitanism.

A more serious problem concerns possible bias introduced by the fact that only about 559,000 of the desired 900,000 questionnaires were returned with enough data to be usable (*ibid.,* p. 557). In addition to the usual problems of "motivated non-compliance" on the level of the individual student, this 38% rate of non-completion is the result of the fact that approximately 30% of the school administrations either refused to cooperate or gave insufficient information. The study itself was the object of much political conflict between federal government officials and major figures in a number of large cities such as Chicago, where it might be expected that inequality according to race would be unusually severe. It would be very difficult to know just what effect these "official" non-responses may have had on the data. Special studies of the "drop-out" schools (*ibid.,* p. 565) show that the difference in average availability of various educational facilities to whites and non-whites should be increased by about 1 percentage point. Since the average availability to the two races was very close to begin with, (74.0% for whites, 72.4% for non-whites), the bias is probably of little significance. Still, the effect of politically motivated non-cooperation remain unknown as to direction and magnitude.

A small follow-up study comparing the students' responses to the "factual" items on the questionnaire with the answers that teachers knew themselves or secured from the parents showed percentages of agreement generally well up into the 90's, while the students themselves exhibited no tendency either to overstate or understate their reports of such items as their previous year's grade average (*ibid.,* pp. 568-570).

The Sub-sample

The Social Relations Department at Harvard was fortunately able to secure copies of the magnetic tapes containing the data of the Coleman Study.

These are organized according to grade, region, and the metropolitan/non-metropolitan dichotomy. "Metropolitan" here means a city of over 50,000 population or its suburbs (*ibid.,* p. 9). On grounds of social and political interest, and because of the greater number of both white and non-white students, the "metropolitan Northeast" sample was selected for use in this and other analyses conducted by faculty and students in the department. This segment of the original data includes the metropolitan schools (and their "feeder" junior high schools) of the District of Columbia, Maryland, Delaware, New Jersey, Pennsylvania, New York, Connecticut, Rhode Island, Massachusetts, New Hampshire, Vermont, and Maine. According to the 1960 Census figures, this region included about 16% of the nation's black children of school age and 20% of the white (*ibid.,* p. 9). By 1965 when the data were collected, the metropolitan Northeast probably contained an even larger proportion of the country's black students.

Ninth-grade students were selected for this analysis of self-conception, race, and family as determinants of major orientation to achievement and life aspiration. Selection of these respondents eliminates as much as possible the systematic bias that occurs when a sample is drawn from students still in school who are over the age (usually 16) of compulsory attendance. The ninth-grade students in Coleman's sample are predominantly aged 14, although a few are as young as 12 and some as old as 19.

The actual respondents in this analysis consist of a 5% systematic subsample of 1,684 ninth-graders, drawn from the complete tape on some 337,000 metropolitan Northeast ninth-graders. All non-blacks have been excluded from the "non-white" category. It should be noted that black students were intentionally over-represented in the Coleman Study in order to provide enough cases for controlled statistical analyses; thus while black children make up 9.6% of all metropolitan Northeast children aged 5 to 19, in our sample 31.2% are black [535 out of 1684] (*ibid.,* p. 39). This will not cause problems in the descriptive findings of this analysis, however, since the reported percentages, and correlations, etc., are in every case separate for each race.

Another study designed to survey American high schools was conducted by Project Talent. It included an investigation of the aptitudes, socioeconomic status, and motivation of students in grades 9 to 12. Comparison of our sample with Project Talent's reveals a close approximation as to the students' father's education and occupation and as to who is the family's breadwinner (Flanagan *et al.,* 1964: 5-22). A comparison of the aspirations of both samples (the student's desire for education, his college plans, and occupational expectation) reveals a close congruence, with slightly more modest aspirations expressed by the students surveyed by Coleman (*ibid.,* pp. 5-21, 25-18).

Specific Variables

A total of twenty variables were selected from the set of more than 100 items of information available on each student. For purposes of cross-tabulation the original scores have been grouped into the ordered categories shown in Figure 2. In all cases the categories were assigned numbers systematically, so that the larger numbers represent positions denoting increasing amounts of whatever continuum is assumed to be involved.

This procedure produces the ordered-categories level of measurement, where there is more inherent order in the categories than those of the typical nominal variable, but less finely discriminated order than in an ordinal variable (in which each unit occupies a unique rank-order position, with a few tied cases). The ordered-category technique has many advantages over nominal categorization, especially in that strength and sign of a relationship between two variables can be expressed thereby with relative ease, precision, and interpretability. In particular, I will be expressing the strengths and signs of the inter-relations between cross-tabulated variables in terms of the measures Tau C and Somers' D. (Couch, *et al.,* 1967: 329-333; Somers, 1962). The formulas for Tau C and for D assume that the categories of both row and column variables are intrinsically ordered on their underlying dimensions (such as "low/medium/high," or "lower-class/working-class/middle-class/upper-middle-class," etc.). Both measures can take on the value of 1.0 for perfect positive association, 0.0 for complete unpredictability and —1.0 for perfect negative association. Neither measure requires that the number of rows in the table be equal to the number of columns.

The measures differ in the dimensionality of their interpretations. Tau C is an appropriate measure with which to express for two ordered-set variables what the product-moment correlation (r) expresses for two continuous-interval variables: the degree of their mutual co-variation. Just as the Pearsonian r is the geometric mean of the two standardized slope coefficients of the two least-squares regression lines (b_{yx} formed when predicting Y from X; and b_{xy}, formed when predicting X from Y), Tau C is one good symmetrical measure of ordered-set mutual association with no presumption that one variable is "causing" the other. When the logic of the analysis does require an interpretation of the presumed "effect" of one "antecedent" ordered-set variable on another seen as a "consequence," the Somers' D measure will be used to express this asymmetric or one-way relation in a manner analogous to b_{yx}, the standardized slope coefficient of the particular regression being referred to in attempts to predict the level of the dependent variable (Y) from knowledge of the independent variable (X).

Whatever measure of association is used in expressing the form and strength of a particular relationship, we also may have some interest in the level of confidence, for it may be that we are observing only the results of fluctuations in random sampling from a population in which the variables are completely unrelated. Therefore, the results of the appropriate test of *in*-significance (x^2 for cross-tabulation, *t* on the *r* for correlation) will be indicated by the presence of one star for the .05 level of significance, two stars for the .01 level, and three stars for $p < .001$ (cross-tabulation only; r's are tested for the .05 and .01 levels only). Thus the notation Tau C = + .40*** means that the two variables are positively related to a relatively strong degree, and that the likelihood that the association occurred by chance is less than one chance in a thousand. The notation r = — .20** means a negative relation, weaker in magnitude, of $p < .01$. Once again, when cross-tabulation measures are used (such as Somers' $D = + .11^{*}$) it means that the chi-square on the table from which it was calculated was significant at the .05 level.

FIGURE 2: Variables, categorizations, and percentage distributions for black and white students, and association of each with race.

INDEPENDENT VARIABLES

Race

1. BLACK STUDENTS		2. WHITE STUDENTS	
31%		69%	(N=1684)

Social Class

Percent		Percent	
25	3. Middle	44	
47	2. Working	45	
28	1. Lower	11	
(517)		(1146)	D=.26***

INTERVENING VARIABLES

Family Role Structure

Percent		Percent	
62	4. Strong Male	86	
28	3. Matriarchy	9	
5	2. Weak Male	3	
5	1. Neither Parent	2	
(525)		(1159)	D=.23***

Parental Aspiration (student reported)

Percent		Percent	
36	3. High (3-4)	36	
31	2. Medium (2)	30	
33	1. Low (0-1)	33	
(525)		(1159)	D=.00

Verbal Ability

Percent		Percent	
23	2. High	64	
77	1. Low (below common median)	36	
(525)		(1159)	D=.40***

SELF-CONCEPTION VARIABLES

Self-Acceptance

Percent		Percent	
49	3. Accepts Self	54	
23	2. Uncertain	24	
29	1. Rejects Self	22	
(431)		(1096)	D=.07*

Self-Rated Brightness

Percent		Percent	
13	5. Among Brightest	14	
23	4. Above Average	30	
43	3. Average	48	
5	2. Below Average	3	
16	1. Blank	5	
(525)		(1159)	D=.14***

Academic Competence

Percent		Percent	
22	3. High	26	
48	2. Medium	44	
29	1. Low	30	
(427)		(1083)	D=.02

Self-Determination

Percent		Percent	
17	3. High	28	
53	2. Medium	50	
30	1. Low	22	
(425)		(1097)	D=.15***

Sensed General Competence

Percent		Percent	
11	3. High	11	
66	2. Medium	66	
22	1. Low	23	
(431)		(1082)	D=—.01

Global Self-esteem

Percent		Percent	
19	3. High	28	
39	2. Medium	37	
42	1. Low	35	
(442)		(1104)	D=.11***

ASPIRATION VARIABLES

How Good a Student the Respondent Wants To Be

Percent		Percent	
55	2. One of best	43	
45	1. Less	57	
(488)		(1137)	D=—.12***

High School Program

Percent		Percent	
22	3. College Prep	41	
31	2. None yet, or doesn't know	17	
46	1. Other program	42	
(525)		(1159)	D=.13***

OVERALL GRADE AVERAGE

Continuous Version

Black		White	
Percent		Percent	
11	4. A's	16	
35	3. B's	46	
25	2. C's	23	
29	1. D's, don't know	15	
(525)		(1159)	D=.20***

Grouped Version

Percent		Percent	
46	2. A's, B's	62	
54	1. Lower	38	
(525)		(1159)	D=.16**

DESIRE FOR EDUCATION

Continuous Version

Percent		Percent	
17	6. Professional or graduate work	20	
32	5. Graduate from 4-year college	34	
30	4. Technical, business, or part of college	26	
14	3. High school only	16	
4	2. Not finish high school	3	
3	1. No answer or don't know	1	
(525)		(1159)	D=.05*

Grouped Version

Percent		Percent	
49	2. B.A. or more	54	
51	1. Less	46	
(525)		(1159)	D=.04

COLLEGE PLANS

Continuous Version

Percent		Percent	
43	4. Definitely yes	46	
34	3. Probably yes	26	
16	2. Probably no	18	
7	1. Definitely no	10	
(504)		(1140)	D=—.01**

Grouped Version

Percent		Percent	
43	2. Definitely yes	46	
57	1. Other	54	
(504)		(1140)	D=.03

OCCUPATIONAL EXPECTATION

Continuous Version

Percent		Percent	
33	7. Executive or professional	42	
3	6. Managerial and ownership	4	
6	5. Technical and sales	7	
5	4. Skilled craftsmen and foreman	7	
9	3. Semi-skilled labor or clerical	10	
0	2. Unskilled labor	1	
44	1. Don't know, blank	29	
(525)		(1159)	D=.15***

Grouped Version

Percent		Percent	
36	3. Professional, business	46	
20	2. Lesser white collar, blue collar	25	
44	1. Uncommitted	29	
(525)		(1159)	D=.15***

Independent Variables

Race was determined by way of the question: "Which of the following best describes you? (A) Negro, (B) White, (C) American Indian, (D) Oriental, (E) Other." For this analysis, the Indians, Orientals, and "Others" have been removed, leaving 1159 white students (69%) and 525 black students (intentionally over-sampled, 31%).

Social Class was indexed by taking into consideration the occupation and education of the student's father, if he were present, or of the student's mother in the remaining cases. To be categorized as "middle-class," a student would have reported his parents' occupation as at least at the technical or sales level of white-collar work, or (much less frequently) that his parents did blue-collar work but had at least some college education. A "working-class" student is one whose parent was reported as being a blue-collar worker with at most a high-school diploma. The "lower-class" category contains the respondent who said he had no working father, or at most a working mother with less than a high-school education.

Intervening Variables

Family role structure was conceptualized as a roughly ordered set of four categories of configuration: "strongly male" which is the culturally ideal situation, "matriarchy," "weak male," and "neither parent."

In order to fall into the "strong male" category a student must report that the real father, or a step- or foster-father, or another male lives in the home and that that male supports the family. His home situation can also be considered "strong male" if he indicates his real father, a step- or foster-father or another male lives in the home and that his *father* has an occupation. It should be noted that in the Coleman Study it would be possible for a child with a "weak father" to be classified as belonging in a "strong male" configuration as we have defined it. If the student states he lives in a household with a male who is not his real father (but who does not provide financial support or have an occupation) but reports an occupation for his father (who may be divorced or separated from his mother) the student *could* fall into the second definition of "strong male" configuration even though a strong male role model is not present. However, inspection of the data reveals small likelihood that this would occur.

"Matriarchy" denotes the family configuration of the student who reports no acting father at home and a real, step- or foster-mother or another female acting as mother in the household.

The household is classified as "weak male" if the real father or a step- or foster-father or other male is present, but someone outside or a female (acting mother) in his household is the source of support. A student can also belong in the "weak male" configuration if he reports a real, a step- or foster-father or another male present in the home, but gives no occupation for his father. This second definition of the "weak male" configuration also suffers from the same defects as the second definition of the "strong male" configuration. It could be the case that a student living in a household with a male (who is not his father but who provides financial support) might indicate no occupation for his father. The strong male role model is indeed present, but it happens not to be the father, whose occupation Coleman's questionnaire requests.

The "neither parent" configuration, the least populated category, defines the family of the student reporting no acting father or acting mother in the home. Presumably this category includes only adolescents in institutions.

These categories of family role structure, ("strong male," "matriarchy," "weak male," "neither parent,") were chosen on the basis of a hypothesis developed in previous work (Gordon and Shea, 1967): that presence of a weak male role model would be even more detrimental to children than would the complete absence of the father. This line of reasoning is built into hypotheses 11 to 14 of the present analysis.

It should be clear that these working definitions of social class and family role structure are *not* completely independent, since reporting the presence of an employed father is enough to disqualify a student from being categorized as "lower-class." However, all the other combinations of social class and family role structure do occur, and the relationships between class and family structure are not so large as to suggest immense contamination. The Somers' D from a social class-family role structure cross-tabulation of blacks is .24** and of whites it is .19**. The Cramer V's of blacks and whites are .28 and .34.

Parental educational aspiration was indexed by the number of times the student *reported* that his parents scored "high" on the following questions: mother wanting him to be "one of the best" students in his class (51%), father wanting the same (51%), mother desiring him to obtain a B.A. or to go to graduate school (56%), and father desiring the same (51%). The size and consistency of the proportion of students reporting that their parents desire these high levels of academic attainment and the close approximation of these reports to other percentages of students reporting a desire to be "one of the best" students in the class (49%) and at least to be a college graduate (52%) suggest that there is probably a good deal of contamination between the two self-reports. However, the distribution of number of times of reported parental urging showed much more variance than such a strict hypothesis of contamination would suggest: no parental urging = 23%; one urging = 10%; two urgings = 30%; three urgings = 8%; four urgings = 29%. The Somers' D's and Cramer V's for parental aspiration with desire for education and plans for college of both blacks and whites are as follows:

	Blacks	*Whites*
Desire for Education	D = .40** Cramer's V = .503	D = .51** Cramer's V = .634
Plans for College	D = .31** Cramer's V = .385	D = .39** Cramer's V = .488

Once again, it should be pointed out that there is some operational overlap between the variable, family role structure, and this index of parents' educational aspiration. Where the student actually has no living parent or only one, he cannot score either 3 or 4 on the index. Yet even among the 5% of the sample who report that neither parent lives in their immediate vicinity, over half report two or more urgings, presumably on the part of the living but absent parents. Furthermore, since some 78% of the students report actually living with both parents, the degree of operational overlap has to be rather small. In fact, the asymmetric Lambda regarding prediction of reported parental aspiration from knowledge of family role structure indicates only a proportional reduction in error of 11% in the case of blacks and 9% in the case of whites.

A wide range of measures of academic ability was used in Coleman's study, including non-verbal and verbal, and assessments of reading, mathematics and general information (1966: 20-21, 218-272, 575-615). However, a complex set of statistical analyses (*ibid.*, pp. 292-295) led the Coleman associates to focus primary attention on the measure of verbal ability. The same procedure will be followed in our study, but a somewhat different interpretation will be placed on the nature of the dimension. Coleman argues that the verbal comprehension score is the best available measure of the student's actual *achievement* or learning to date, rather than being primarily an estimate of some more general *capacity* to learn. He thus attempts to use it to assess the differential impact of a wide range of school-related factors, although he clearly recognizes that longitudinal measures of change in this or other capacities would be a more valid indicator (*ibid.*, p. 292). Since we are not concerned at present with the complex determinants of developed mental capacity, the verbal ability score will simply be taken as one possible index of this very important capacity, whatever the roots of its development.

The over-all measure of *verbal ability* was composed of sixty items from the Educational Testing Service's *School and College Ability Tests* (p. 581). Thirty questions, to be answered in a maximum of fifteen minutes, were sentence-completions designed to test verbal comprehension, such as:

High yields of food crops per acre accelerate the ______________ of soil nutrients.

(A) depletion
(B) erosion
(C) cultivation
(D) fertilization
(E) conservation

Another thirty items for which ten minutes was allowed, tested verbal comprehension with synonyms:

Necessitate
(A) make essential
(B) continue indefinitely
(C) vibrate
(D) compete
(E) barely

Chilly
(A) tired
(B) nice
(C) dry
(D) cold
(E) sunny

Obviously (and as Coleman clearly points out on p. 20), this mode of measuring verbal ability is in no sense culture free. It clearly rewards the academic fluency that continues to be of great importance in obtaining high grades, getting into college, and gaining entrance to what are called the "highest occupations."

Although the Coleman Report gives no details of the ways in which the machine-recorded answers were combined numerically to form the overall verbal ability score, the resulting distribution in our sample of 1684 urban Northeast ninth-graders rather well approximates the normal curve, having the following properties:

Highest score = 321	Mean = 269.3	SD = 15.8	Skewness = 0.11
Lowest score = 239	Median = 269.0	Kurtosis = 0.63	

As is shown in Figure 2, for purposes of cross-tabulation this measure was dichotomized at the median, 269, a procedure which sacrifices a great deal of information contained in the continuous variable, but comparison of subgroups according to percentages at or above the common median concisely clarifies the rather strong findings. Later correlation and path coefficient analyses will utilize the full range of scores on this index of verbal ability.

Self-Conception Variables

The Coleman study was unusual in that it included a number of questions relevant to various aspects of self-conception.

Basic self-acceptance was inferred from a single question: "If I could change, I would be someone different from myself—'agree,' 'not sure,' 'disagree.' " The figure of 24% indicating self-rejection is in close accord with the outcomes of Coleman's earlier study of some 7,000 Illinois high school students (1961:220-236).

Self-rated brightness is also assessed from a single item: "How bright do you think you are in comparison with the other students in your grade?—'among the brightest,' 'above average,' 'average,' 'below the average,' or 'among the lowest.' " The few respondents selecting the last two categories have been combined in the cross-tabulations. The 42% checking 'above average' or 'one of the brightest' corresponds very closely with the pattern for the nation (12 + 35 = 47%). It should be remembered, however, that our percentage may be altered slightly by the oversampling of black students.

Sensed academic competence is similar to what the Coleman analysts called simply "self-concept," (*ibid*., p. 281-288), but it is indexed from the answers to "I sometimes feel that I just can't learn" and "I would do better in school if the teachers didn't go so fast," without including the self-rated question on brightness. This latter item was deleted from the index because it deals with a much more general competence than the two specifically school-related questions, and it seemed quite likely that numerous students would rate themselves as high on brightness but low on the academic item. The data support this contention, in that self-rated brightness correlates only .16 with "sometimes I just can't learn," only .19 with "teachers go so fast," and .23 with the combined academic competence index.

Most of the multi-item indices used in this analysis were constructed through use of what I have been calling the indicator-mean procedure (Gordon, 1968b), and will be illustrated by reference to the self-determination index.

Sense of self-determination is one of four dimensions that I have suggested as intermediate in generality between the concrete self-descriptions elicited by the "Who am I?" or other free-response tchniques and the more global and inferential sense of personal autonomy and self-esteem (Gordon, 1966; 1968a). Each of the four systemic senses of self is held to be the individual's subjective interpretation of his situation in relation to one of the major problems he faces. The sense of competence is held to be his interpretation of the problem of adaptation, self-determination corresponds to goal-attainment, unity to integration, and the sense of moral worth to pattern-maintenance. Naturally these relationships cannot simply be asserted; they must provide theoretical orientation for a rigorous and hopefully conclusive analysis of relevant empirical data.

Coleman's data contain a number of variables that can be considered as meaningful indicators of the sense of self-determination. These include the three items that he and his associates look upon as reflecting the student's sense of control over his environment (1966:288-290), plus three additional, equally relevant items. Each item was originally presented in an "agree/not sure/disagree" format. A value of 1 was assigned to the answer representing the lower amount of felt self-determination, a 2 was assigned to "not sure" and the value 3 was assigned to the most self-determined answer. Respondents omitting information on particular indicators were not scored so as to equal the sample's modal answer (as was done by the Coleman analysts). By the indicator-mean procedure, index scores are calculated by taking the mean of the available indicator values, then subtracting 1.0, multiplying by 10.0, and rounding to yield a set of integer values with a range of 0 for the lowest possible score to 20 for the highest. Since missing indicator values do not enter the calculation of the mean indicator score, the effect of each present indicator is increased in proportion to the amount of missing data. Naturally, the investigator should establish some reasonable minimum number of indicators so that the resulting score will not be based on just a very small fragment of the desired data. In this context, a minimum of 5 out of the 7 included indicators was established, thus eliminating 28 students who had from one to four available indicators, plus 24 respondents who had left all seven blank. There was no need to assign scores to the 28 cases having 5 indicators or to the 54 having 6 indicators, as would have been necessary in most other procedures to construct an index.

There are at least three reasons why the indicator-mean procedure is superior to the technique of simply adding up the raw indicator values. First, it preserves the respondent's pattern of answers by slightly increasing the contribution of each of the available indicators, and does not resort to "manufacturing" answers that he might have given if he were typical of the sample as a whole. We have good reasons to infer that he is not. Second, the practice of subtracting 1.0 from the mean of the available indicator values insures that all indices calculated in this manner will (like all physical measurements involving counting or applications of an interval) start with 0 as the lowest possible particular index. In contrast, additive index scoring usually produces lowest-possible values equal to the particular number of indicators used. Finally, the procedure of rounding the scale scores to the nearest integer produces a convenient set of possible scores (in this case 0 to 20) that does not pretend to the meaningless but apparently precise strategy of discriminating between scores differing only in the first decimal place. Of course, both the indicator-mean procedure and additive reading assume that each step in the item scores is equally large, and that each item is of equal importance. The indicator-mean procedure can be adjusted to allow item weighting if necessary, and factor loadings of the items on the general factor might well be used for this purpose if they are available. In any case, the using of more powerful analytic methods seems worth the risk of violating the equal-interval assumption. Where the error is substantial, it will be likely to reduce differences between groups and thus have a conservative effect on the drawing of inferences.

The specific questions making up the self-determination index and the result of these operations can be seen by examining the questions in order of their part-whole correlation with the total index scores:

	Self-determination Index Item	*Item/Total Correlation*
(—)	Every time I try to get ahead, something or somebody stops me	.53
(—)	People like me don't have much of a chance to be successful in life	.45
(+)	The tougher the job, the harder I work	.44
(—)	Good luck is more important than hard work for success	.42
(+)	If a person is not successful in life, it is his own fault	.42
(—)	People who accept their condition in life are happier than those who try to change things	.33
(+)	I would make any sacrifice to get ahead in life	.29

Although one could easily quibble with these items with their all too obvious orientation toward success and achievement—as against creativity or other forms of autonomy—they do at least on the face of it suggest the possibility of an active, self-directing rejection of control by fate, other people, or social conditions external to the individual (cf. Rotter, 1966).

The resulting distribution of self-determination index scores extends over the completing scoring range, and again forms a rather good approximation to the theoretical normal curve:

Highest score = 20	Mean = 12.8	SD = 3.1	Skewness = −.11
Lowest score = 0	Median = 13.0	Kurtosis = −.06	

While these point scores will be used in the path analysis, for purposes of cross-tabulation the index was trichotomized at the first and third quartiles to yield an additional "low/medium/high" ordered-set variable.

In the *sensed general competence* index an attempt is made to combine the broader self-rated "brightness" measure and the single item "I am able to do many things well" into one dimension with which to approximate the still more general systemic sense of competence referred to above (Gordon, 1968a). The trichotomy shown in Figure 2 was formed by a judgmental combination of the two items. "High" means a simultaneous self-rating as 'one of the brightest' and 'agree' to the assertion of being able to do many things well. "Low" means 'average or less' and 'uncertain or disagreeing.' "Medium" was assigned to all the intermediate combinations, except the 171 cases that lacked information on one or both indicators.

Global Self-esteem

As was indicated at the outset of this brief outline of dimensions of self-conception, the global evaluative dimension (self-esteem) is held to be more comprehensive and general than any of the particular elements such as social identities, body images, the sense of competence, of self-determination, of unity, or of moral worth, of personal autonomy, etc., on which the overall sense of worth might be based. An extensive body of theoretical literature supports this contention (especially the works of James, Cooley, Fromm, Sullivan, Erikson, Rogers, and Shibutani, many of which are collected in Gordon and Gergen, 1968). Unfortunately, there has been relatively little empirical research comprehensively operationalizing self-esteem (noteworthy exceptions being Kardiner and Ovesey, 1951; Cohen, 1959; Sears and Sherman, 1964; Rosenberg, 1965; Coopersmith, 1967).

While there was no direct self-esteem scale included in the Coleman questionnaires, it was possible to use the general theoretical scheme outlined above to provide a rationale for combining the four previously-described measures into a single global index of self-esteem. Competence is represented in both academic and general forms; self-determination has its own index; and the basic self-acceptance variable is taken as, at best, a rough amalgam of the senses of unity and moral worth. In order of descending part-whole correlation with the overall self-esteem index, the constituent elements are:

.68 Academic competence index
.65 Self-determination index
.64 Basic self-acceptance
.49 General competence index

When the trichotomized versions of each of the above components are combined through the indicator-mean procedure, the resulting distribution of self-esteem falls in a nicely balanced spread of scores slightly flatter than a perfect normal curve and with the following characteristics:

Highest score = 20	Mean = 10.5	SD = 4.8	Skewness = −.06
Lowest score = 0	Median = 10.0	Kurtosis = .71	

Trichotomization of these scores for the cross-tabulation analysis yields an ordered-set global self-esteem score on which 42% are categorized as low, 39% medium, and 19% as high among the black students, and 35% as low, 37% as medium, and 28% as high among the whites.

Now that the related aspects of self-conception have been described in both theoretical and operational terms, it remains to be shown that they are related but not identical dimensions. Figure 3 presents the zero-order correlations among the full continuous versions of these self-conception variables.

Disregarding the circled correlations (which are expected to be high by virtue of being part-whole relations of a variable with one of its relatively small number of constituent elements), a number of conclusions are suggested by the remaining correlation patterns. First, the frequent substantial differences in the intercorrelations indicate that these measures of self-conception are not arbitrary or random variates. Second, the five separate dimensions are not merely alternative operationalizations of each other (the average intercorrelation is +.13 for blacks and +.20 for whites) and the highest is only +.26, indicating less than 7% shared variance). Third, the argument that basic self-acceptance is likely to be based on much more than sensed individual competence gains support from the fact that self-rated brightness and the measure of abstract general competence of which it is a part each correlate only +.06 with self-acceptance for blacks and +.10** for whites.

Figure 3—Intercorrelations among self-conception dimensions, within the racial groups. Circled values are part-whole correlations.

VARIABLE		1. B	1. W	2. B	2. W	3. B	3. W	4. B	4. W	5. B	5. W	Aver. of Uncircled Correls.
1. **BASIC SELF-ACCEPTANCE**	Black											.15
	White											.16
2. SELF-RATED BRIGHTNESS	Black	.01										.06
	White		.13**									.19
3. ACADEMIC COMPETENCE	Black	.25**		.09								.16
	White		.23**		.29**							.26
4. GENERAL COMPETENCE	Black	.06		(.63)		.08						.09
	White		.10**		(.66)		.23**					.18
5. SELF-DETERMINATION	Black	.27**		.07		.22**		.13**				.17
	White		.19**		.15**		.31**		.20**			.21
6. GLOBAL SELF-ESTEEM	Black	(.68)		(.26)		(.66)		(.43)		(.62)		-
	White		(.62)		(.41)		(.70)		(.51)		(.65)	-

Grand Average r:
Blacks: .13
Whites: .20

This is in contrast with the stronger relation of self-acceptance to the dimension representing connection to the more immediate social environment (+.25** and +.23** with academic competence). Fourth, it is encouraging to discover (as in previous work, Gordon, 1968c) that sensed freedom from control by the social environment stands in just as strong a relation to basic self-acceptance (+.27** and +.19** with sensed self-determination).

Taken together, the composition of these self-conception indices and the pattern of their interrelationships seem sufficient to support a moderate but cautious confidence in their validity and meaningfulness.

Aspiration and Achievement

Six aspects of aspiration to future achievement or actual recent achievement were included in the Coleman questionnaires. Together, they encompass the major range of dimensions generally dealt with in the literature on aspiration (recently summarized by Slocum, 1966:ch. 9-11; Goldstein, 1967:ch. 2-4; and Osipow, 1968). Several additional variables were included that give greater substance to the picture of achievement-related factors and broaden the time-frame under consideration.

Aspiration to academic attainment in the school concerns a pattern of orientation toward achievement within the immediate social environment, one which is little explored in a literature focused primarily on a distant and misty future. Coleman's questionnaires included the question: "How good a student do you want to be in school,"—'one of the best students in my class,' 'above the middle of the class,' 'in the middle of my class,' 'just good enough to get by,' and 'I don't care.' " Fully 47% of the ninth-graders in this sample checked 'one of the best,' and only 59 students left the question blank. Anything less than the highest performance was collapsed into a single category for cross-tabulation analysis (53%).

School program is a concrete embodiment of both educational and occupational aspiration. Enrollment in the college preparatory program is also an all but bureaucratically necessary—though not sufficient—step toward eventually going to college, establishing, as it does, the context of classroom and extracurricular interaction with college-oriented students. Unless very vigorous change is accomplished before the junior year (11th grade), entrance into a blue-collar or at best a minor white-collar occupation is almost a certainty. Even though these students are only about fourteen years old, this single decision concerning school program (made by them, their parents, and, perhaps, by school officials) will have an immense impact on their entire lives. Just two-thirds of these students are still in a junior high school (in areas where grades 10 to 12 are high school), yet only 31% of the black students and 17% of the white students left a blank or wrote in "don't know" in response to the question "Which one of the following best describes the program or curriculum you are enrolled in?"—'General,' 'college preparatory,' 'commercial or business,' 'vocational,' 'agricultural,' 'industrial arts,' 'other.' " The "don't knows" were placed in the intermediate position on the school program variable while the 22% blacks and 41% whites indicating that they were enrolled in the college preparatory program were placed in the "high" position. Those who gave any of the other programs as answers (46% of the black sample and 42% of the white sample) were placed in the first or "low" category.

Over-all grade average was requested in a straightforward self-report question: "What is your grade average for all your school work?—'A', 'B', 'C', 'D', 'don't know.' " A special validity study (N = 700) conducted by Coleman and his associates indicated that this item elicited self-reports identical with a direct coding from school records in 93.6% of the cases (p. 570). In one sense this over-all grade average could be viewed as a measure of the student's mental or at least academic capacity, but only if we ignored all we know about the large range of factors that shape academic achievement. It seems preferable to regard this rough grade average as an outome of the *application* of mental capacity and a great many other techniques such as diligence, conventionally, neatness, etc. Thus it can be seen as a kind of achievement to date within the immediate academic realm. It should be noted that 29% of the black and 15% of the white students, the categories in lowest position on the variable, include some students who left the question blank and some who indicated that they did not know what their grade average was, together with those who admitted to an over-all D average. This procedure is based on the reasoning that grades are so crucial in American secondary schools that students not answering this question or responding, "don't know," are quite likely to be evading an unpleasant truth.

Desire for education is one of the most commonly investigated of the aspirations that fall toward the fantasy end of the scale of projected self-images. The question was "How far do you want to go in school?"—'I do not want to finish high school,' 'I want to finish high school only,' 'I want to go to technical, nursing, or business school, after high school,' 'Some college training but less than four years,' 'I want to graduate from a four-year college,' 'I want to do professional or graduate work after I finish college.' " It is hoped that the emphasis on the word "want" focuses the students' attention on the level of desired education and is more realistic than questions such as "If things could be just the way you would like them to be, how much education would you *ideally like* to eventually complete?" It still allows somewhat more scope for aspiration than does Coleman's question: "Are you planning to go to college (junior or four-year college)?—'definitely yes,' 'probably yes,' 'probably not,' 'definitely not.' " The responses to these questions will be used in the form in which they are shown in Figure 2 for the path analyses, but for purposes of convenient cross-tabulation, each has been dichotomized at the indicated points. Thus while 49% of the black and 54% of the white students indicate at least completion of college as their desire, only 42% of the black and 46% of the whites say that they definitely plan to go to college. Of course, it may be argued that none of these levels of educational aspiration make much real sense in the light of the fact that these are only ninth-graders answering a paper-and-pencil questionnaire and not in a real situation. Yet this is always the case with research on aspiration; only such ephemeral expressions of orientation toward possible future courses of action are being tapped. More full-scale longitudinal research is imperative if we are ever to untangle the threads of fantasy, desire, intention and planning that weave present conduct from the futures of the past. (Flanagan *et al.,* 1962, 1964, Flanagan and Cooley, 1966; Duncan, Haller and Portes, 1968).

Occupational expectation takes us even further into our own speculation about the meaning of a student's speculation about a line of conduct far removed in time from the present. Yet once again it is known that such long-term projects of action as occupational ambition do provide the students' immediate selection of means to these ends much of their basic orientation and meaning (Schutz, 1932: esp. ch. 2). Furthermore, it is probably true that the first major occupations they engage in when in their twenties will be roughly the same or will rank only a little lower in status than the occupations that they now give in answer to Coleman's question: "When you finish your education, what sort of a job do you think you will have?" Ten categories of occupations were listed, with many concrete examples of each: technical; official; manager, proprietor or owner; semi-skilled worker, clerical worker, service worker, protective worker; salesman; farm or ranch manager or owner; farm worker; workman or laborer; professional; skilled worker or foreman; and 'don't know.' Figure 2 shows the occupations categorized by rank order of status, with the percentage indicating each. The rough connection between aspiration and actuality is the result of the effect on both of the present social-class position of the student's parents, coupled with the prevalent rather short upward mobility from the parental starting point (Blau and Duncan, 1967: chapter 2). Thus while the actual specific content of the occupation entered may differ greatly according to a qualitative framework, it is quite probable that the status ranking of that occupation will match, or fall somewhat short of, that expressed in our six grouped clusters, and this probability is increased if we consider only the gross disparity between the 36% blacks and 46% whites who say they expect to have a professional or managerial career and the 20% blacks and 25% whites (after we had removed those who did not give a definite answer) who expect to enter a lesser white-collar or blue-collar job.

The intercorrelations of these dimensions of achievement and aspiration (Figure 4) show some interesting patterns. These variables are more closely associated than were the dimensions of self-conception (average correlation = .26 for blacks and .35 for whites, ranging from a low of .15 between aspiration to attainment in the present school and occupational expectation of blacks and .24 between aspiration to academic attainment and high school program of whites, to a high of .47 in the case of blacks and .71 in the case of whites between amount of education said to be desired and the more realistic plans for college). Occupational expectation is most highly correlated with desire among whites for education (.43**) and with overall grade average among blacks (.33**). The fact that the variable, desired education, has the highest average intercorrelation with the other aspirations of both blacks (.31) and whites (.46) and the further fact that the literature gives prominence to the desire for education led us to structure much of our analysis around this particularly important aspect of adolescent orientation. Once again, the pattern of intercorrelation is seen to be quite different between the

Figure 4—Intercorrelations among the achievement and aspiration dimensions, within the racial groups.

VARIABLE		1. B W	2. B W	3. B W	4. B W	5. B W	Average of Correlations
1. ACADEMIC ATTAINMENT ASP.	Black						.21
	White						.33
2. SCHOOL PROGRAM	Black	.25**					.26
	White	.24**					.32
3. OVER-ALL GRADE AVERAGE	Black	.19**	.22**				.24
	White	.34**	.29**				.35
4. DESIRE FOR EDUCATION	Black	.29**	.31**	.22**			.31
	White	.42**	.40**	.36**			.46
5. COLLEGE PLANS	Black	.29**	.20**	.22**	.47**		.29
	White	.39*	.34**	.37**	.71**		.45
6. OCCUPATION EXPECTATION	Black	.15**	.30**	.33**	.27**	.16**	.24
	White	.26**	.34**	.36**	.43**	.40**	.36

Grand Average r:
Black: .26
White: .35

races—in every one of the 15 comparisons the blacks show the lower correlation, averaging .26 in contrast to the whites' .35.

This set of concrete achievements (school program and grade average to date) plus aspirations to academic attainment in high school, desired amount of education, presence and certainty of plans for college, and some rough idea of expected occupation provide a wide range of relevant dimensions. Serious logical and pragmatic criticisms can be raised against each particular procedure, and, indeed, against each underlying concept. Yet the worthwhileness of the attempt to explore the independent and joint effects of structure, family, individual capacity and self-conception in the wide domain of aspiration to achievement can be assessed only in terms of its demonstration of important empirical relations among the variables. Demonstration and analysis of these relations form the core of the following sections.

IV

IV. ANALYSIS OF THE DATA

One might begin to test our explicit hypotheses by entering zero-order correlation coefficients on the appropriate arrows of the theoretical model of Figure 1. The signs and values of such correlation coefficients would have a rough but interpretable meaning, because on each of the variables, as has been noted, the larger numerical values represent increasing amounts of the property being tapped. Actually, a distinct set of these correlations would have to be supplied for every unique combination of alternative measures under the rubrics, self-conception and aspiration, or some form of summary index would have to be constructed to represent each set of factors. While "global self-esteem" can be used for self-conception, I was reluctant to do this kind of summarizing in the case of the diverse forms of aspiration, and so I selected only the variable, desire for education, with which to construct the zero-order model shown in Figure 5. Correlations are given separately by race because the black students were oversampled in the Coleman Study. Relations 1, 3, 5, 7, and 9 involve race directly and the correlations are given for rough reference only, since they understate the true relations.

On the basis of these statistically significant and generally substantial correlations, one might be tempted to conclude that 17 of the 20 hypotheses have gained solid support. Only three of them were not confirmed: relation 3, where the value $r = +.003$, indicates that white parents are *not* more likely to be reported as urging educational achievement and going to college (an

Figure 5—Zero-order correlations between the indicated pairs of variables in the hypothesized model. The numbered arrows correspond to the hypotheses in Section II; "B" indicates a correlation for black students, "W" for white students. For variables correlated with race, the single correlation indicated is conservative due to minimized variance caused by oversampling of black students.

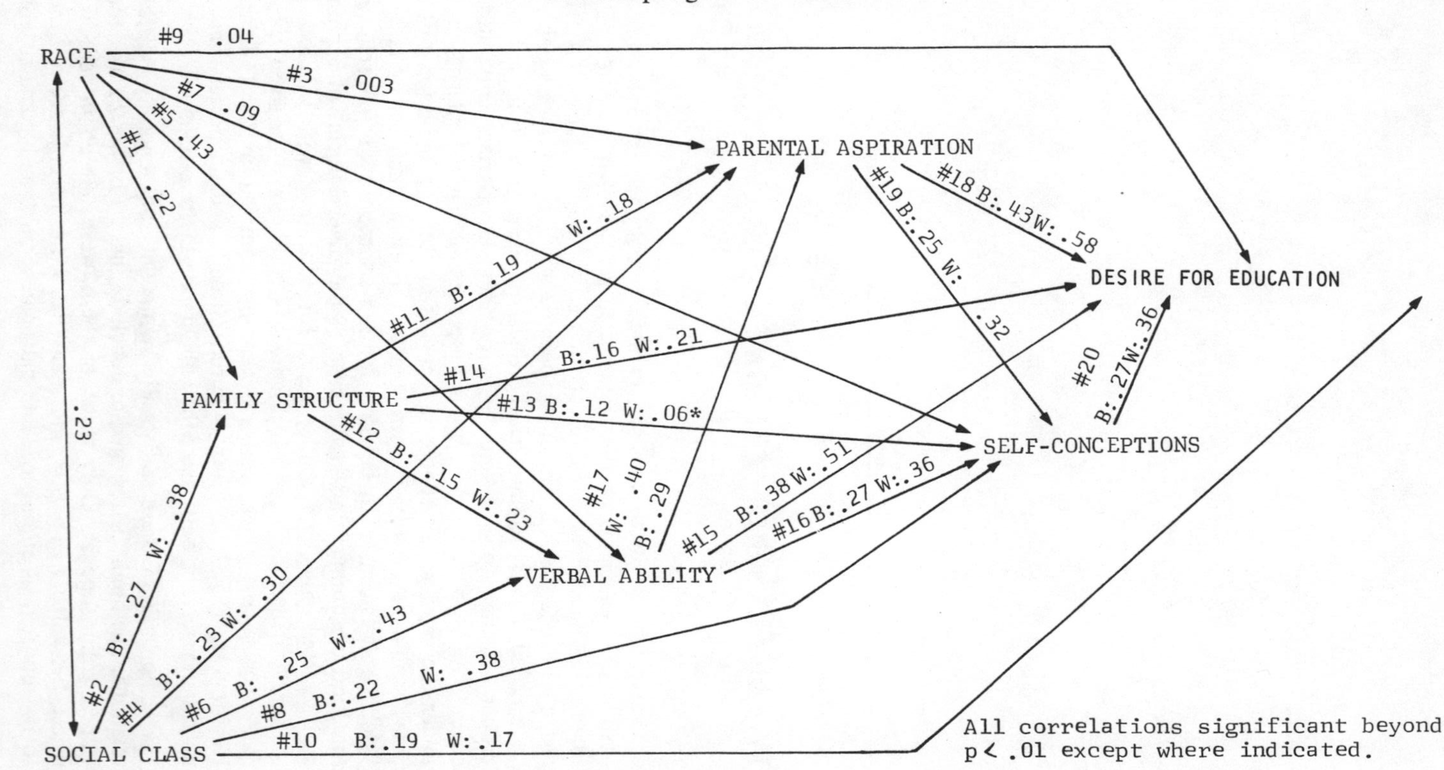

outcome anticipated by the cautionary note to the hypothesis; relation 7, where whites seem to have only very slightly more favorable self-conceptions; and relation 9, where the value $r = .04$ tells us that, contrary to prediction, white students are slightly *more* likely to desire college or graduate education. All the other correlations are quite unlikely ($p<.01$) to be the result of sampling fluctuation in a population in which there is actually a zero correlation between the relevant variables.

Yet even such substantial correlations as #15, the $r = .51^{**}$ for whites between parents' aspiration and their desire for their children's education, the $r = .43^{**}$ between race and verbal ability, or the $r = .36^{**}$ for whites between global self-esteem and aspiration, can be very misleading. Correlation coefficients express only the degree of mutual interrelation between a particular *pair* of variables, without taking account of any other variables that may be affecting both. Thus, as is well known, a high zero-order correlation between two variables may be a spurious reflection of the fact that both are actually influenced by a shared causal antecedent. Conversely, small zero-order correlations may be the result of the fact that two or more subgroups in the sample (according to position or some third variable) have relations of approximately equal magnitude but opposite sign, thus cancelling each other out in cases where only the two immediate variables are considered.

There are more advanced multivariate techniques for evaluating the partial or unique relation between any given pair of variables. Path analysis will be used for that purpose and also for assessing the entire theoretical model at once. Yet a more direct and intuitive understanding of the robustness of particular relations after taking account of possible prior determinants can often be obtained through close examination of appropriately controlled cross-tabulations. Therefore, with this more familiar form of data analysis and display we will lay the groundwork required before the more powerful method can be employed with confidence.

RACE AND CLASS AS INDEPENDENT VARIABLES

Hypotheses 1 and 2: Race, Social Class and Family Structure

First, let us consider the validity of the major premise of the Moynihan argument:

> Indices of dollars of income, standards of living, and years of education deceive. The gap between the Negro and most other groups in American society is widening.
>
> The fundamental problem, in which this is most clearly the case, is that of family structure. The evidence—not final, but powerfully persuasive—is that the Negro family in the urban ghettos is crumbling. A middle-class group has managed to save itself, but for vast numbers of the unskilled, poorly educated city working class the fabric of conventional social relationships has all but disintegrated. There are indications that the situation may have been arrested in the past few years, but the general post-war trend is unmistakable. So long as this situation persists, the cycle of poverty and disadvantage will continue to repeat itself. (1965:43).

Are the absent father and the patterns of the weak male role in the family's economic structure really "Negro problems"? While it is true that in our sample of urban Northeast ninth-graders 33% of the black students reported that there was no one at home acting as father as against only 11% among the whites reporting the same situation (a ratio of 3:1), there is also an effect of social class that must be extricated from the relationship. In these data, the father is absent in 45% of the lower-class homes, as compared to 14% and 11% of homes of the working and middle class. Since we have observed an understated correlation of roughly +.23 (D = +.26***) between race and class, we are led to examine the prevalence of absent fathers among the joint race-and-class categories. Figure 6 presents the proportion of families lacking a father within each race-and-class category (the working- and middle-class groups have been combined since their patterns of relation in this instance were very similar). It should be noted that in the present sample, 28% of the black students were classified as lower-class, with 47% working-class and 25% middle-class. Among the white students, these categorizations were 12% lower-class, 45% working-class, and 43% middle-class. Thus the blacks were about as likely to be of the working class, but roughly twice as frequently considered lower-class and only about half as likely to be seen as middle-class.

First, as Moynihan asserted, the absent father is much commoner among lower-class blacks than among working- and middle-class blacks (.52 to .25, a ratio of 2.1:1). While the corresponding proportions are substantially lower among whites, the degree of imbalance between the classes is even greater (.37 of the lower class to .08 of the working- and middle-classes, a ratio of 4.6:1).

Figure 6—Proportion reporting father-absence, according to race and social class.

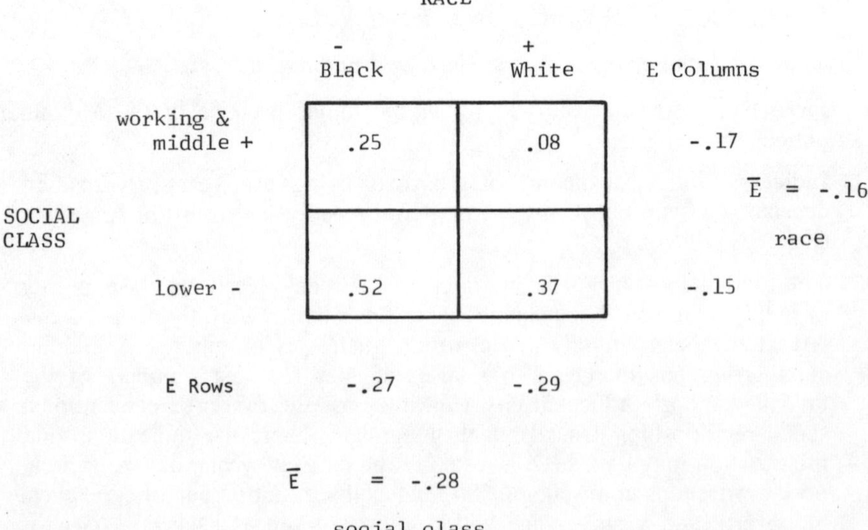

A further inference can be drawn by examining the Epsilons (or differences between two proportions obtained by subtracting the value of the "minus" or "low" side from the value of the "plus" or "high" side across each row and column) and by comparing the resulting average row and column Epsilons. Of course, this procedure is only a very rough approximation to the logic of a 2×2 factorial analysis of variance. It is obvious that the technique of comparing the individual and average Epsilons, calculated from proportions scoring in some defined manner on a nominal dependent variable within the intersected categories of two dichotomized independent variables, completely ignores the problems of differing cell variances and cell sizes. Nevertheless, comparison of the average Epsilons does yield a rough impression of the relative magnitude of the "row effects" (social class) and "column effects" (race). Examination of the separate Epsilons also allows detection of various effects of interaction, although elaborate measures of "significance" are neither provided nor warranted.

This approximation of the Epsilons to a 2×2 analysis of variance can be demonstrated by reference to Figure 6. The column Epsilons of −.17 for working- and middle-class students and −.15 for lower-class students show that the relation of race to prevalence of absent father is very similar regardless of class, that it is negative in sign (the blacks or "lows" in both classes have higher rates), and that the relation is low in magnitude (E columns, the arithmetic average of the column Epsilons, equals only —.16). The row or social-class effects are estimated by the Epsilons of −.27 for blacks and −.29 for whites. Again the size and sign are the same, indicating that there is no appreciable interaction effect: regardless of race, the lower-class students more frequently report the absence of the father. However, the fact that the average Epsilon for social class is more than one and a half times that for race (−.28 to −.16) leads to the conclusion that social class is a more powerful determinant of the father's absence than is race.

Taken together, social class and race are highly predictive of the fatherless family (52% among black lower-class students as against 8% among white working- and middle-class students; a ratio of 6.5:1).

Moreover, the bottom row of Figure 6 reveals two facts of social and political importance. First, the fact that at least 52% of lower-class black ninth-graders represented by the sample are without a father suggests that Moynihan's estimate that some 23% of all non-white families are matriarchal has seriously *underestimated* the magnitude of an explosive urban problem. Second, the fact that at least 37% of the *white* lower-class students are without fathers may eventually have even greater social impact, because of the much larger absolute number of white children living at the poverty level. Although comparison between a single-area sample and national data is difficult and at best very rough, a few key figures may indicate the scope of the problem. Estimates for the relevant time period (1966) are that approximately 29.7 million persons in the United States (about 15% of the total population) were living below the Social Security Administration's definition of the poverty level, $3335 per year for an urban family of four. While it is true that a much higher *proportion* of non-white fell below the line than did whites (about 41% to 12%), it is also true that approximately 20.3 million or 68% of the very poor were whites as compared to 9.3 million (32%) non-whites (National Advisory Commission on Civil Disorders, 1968:258). If father's absence entails the consequences often attributed to it, then the situation is indeed desperate.

When we use a concept of family role structure that is more complicated than definition in terms of the simple presence or absence of a father figure, we find that race and class again combine to weave an intricate pattern. Figure 7 presents the joint relation of race and social class to a four-category

Figure 7—Family role structure according to race and social class.

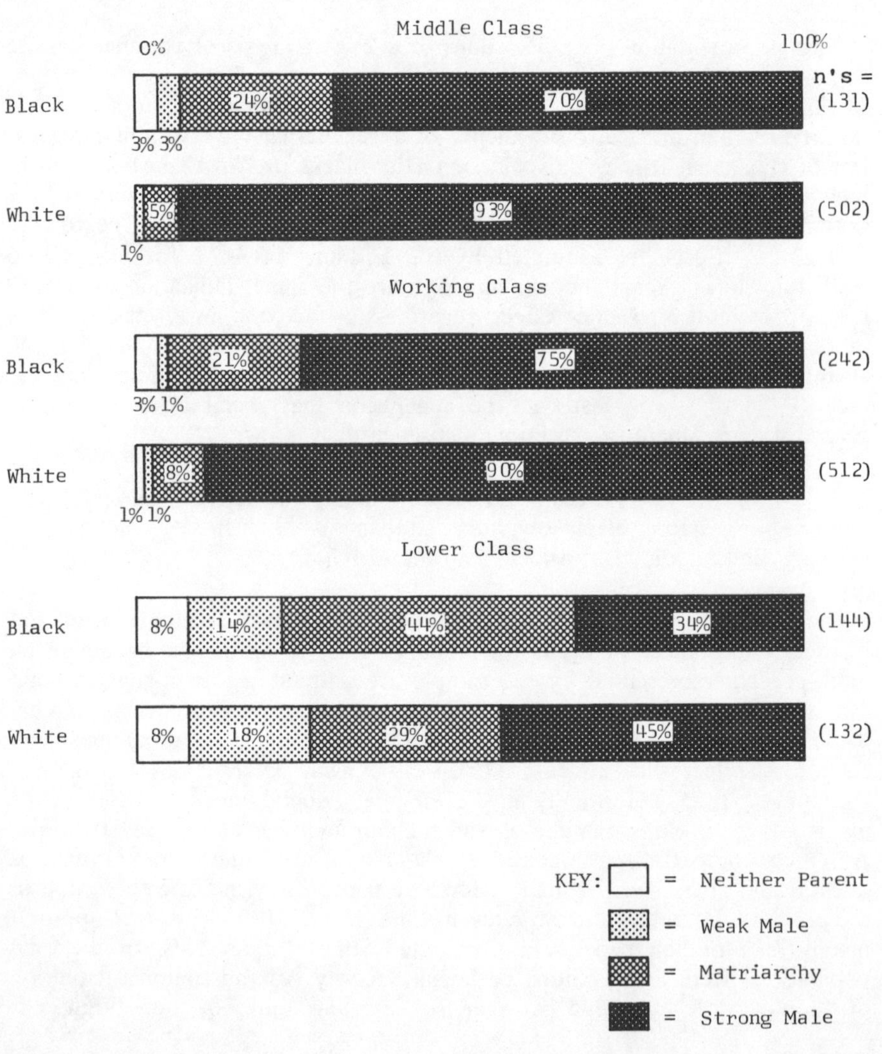

ordered-set variable designed to represent increasing approximation to the cultural ideal of a complete set of parents with the father supplying the strong model of the role of the family provider.

The distribution of the types of family role structure is quite similar in the middle- and working-class and between the races within each class: some 90% or more of the whites report living in families where a father, stepfather, or grandfather provides support; 5% and 8% of the whites as compared to 24% and 21% of the blacks report that only a mother, stepmother, or grandmother supports the family; very small percentages of these middle- and working-class students of either race report living in homes where a male is present but not working or where there is no parental figure.

The black lower-class students are most likely to report that they live with the mother only or other mother figure (44%, as against 29% for the lower-class whites). Only 34% of the blacks and 45% of the white lower-class students report a "strong" male provider at home, while 14% of the blacks and 18% of the whites report a father figure who does not support the family. Finally, 8% of each race among the lower-class students report neither a father nor a mother figure at home. By definition, in such families the primary source of income is some form of public welfare assistance, the programs of which commonly do not tolerate the presence of an able-bodied male. This suggests that an unemployed white father is more likely to be on disability relief but still present, while a black father is more likely to be unemployed even though healthy. Thus the black father, pressed by the rule that there should be no "man in the house," may relinquish his domestic role and leave home so that his wife and children may receive some form of aid (National Advisory Commission on Civil Disorders, 1968:457-467).

Race—Taken together, the data in Figure 7 and the tables from which they were drawn provide support for hypothesis 1, that black students more often have broken or weak-male families than do whites (52% to 23%, a ratio of 2.3:1, Somers' D = .23***).

Class—Hypothesis 2 asserts that working-class students are more likely than those of the middle-class to belong in broken or weak-father families. The lower-class students are omitted from this hypothesis, because the definition of "lower class" used in this study precludes there being a working father; thus the hypothesized relation would be tautological rather than empirical.

Among the black students, the incidence of broken or weak-male families does differ by a small amount according to social class, but the difference is opposite in direction to that hypothesized (25% in the working class, 31% in the middle class). The middle-class black students also show a somewhat higher frequency of the "mother only" pattern than do the working-class blacks (24% to 21%). Among the white students the class difference in incidence of broken family or weak-father configurations again contradicts the proposition, but it is quite insignificant in size (10% in the working class, 7% in the middle class).

These findings might be interpreted as reflecting the fact that the difficulties faced by a black man in trying to fill the dominant role opposite a wife who is working at white-collar, semi-professional or even full professional level are much greater than those of a white father facing the same situation. Thus it must be concluded that hypothesis 2 fails, in that the data of this sample show no tendency for the incidence of broken or weak-father families to be more frequent in the working class than in the middle class, black or white.

To summarize the analysis so far: lower-class position is so strongly associated with a weak paternal role or with complete family disruption that differences between working- and middle-class patterns are overshadowed, and this pattern is nearly as malignantly strong among whites as among blacks. The effects of a man's not fulfilling what is expected of him as a breadwinner have perhaps been delineated best by Elliot Liebow in *Tally's Corner* (1966:108, 109-110, 135-136), in brief passages that may bring to life the general trends portrayed above:

> But as the man on the street corner looks at the reality of marriage as it is experienced day in and day out by husbands and wives, his universe tells him that marriage does not work. He knows that it did not for his own mother and father and for the parents of most of his contemporaries.
>
> * * *
>
> These are the things he sees and hears and knows of street-corner marriage: the disenchantment, sometimes bitter, of those who were or still are married; the public and private fights between husband and wife and the sexual jealousy that rages around them; husbands who cannot feed, clothe, and house their wives and children and husbands who have lost the will to do so; the terror of husband and wife who suddenly find themselves unable to ward off attacks on the health and safety of their children. Nor is there—to redeem all this even in part—a single marriage among the street-corner men and their women which they themselves recognize as a "good" marriage.
>
> * * *
>
> Thus, marriage is an occasion of failure. To stay married is to live with your failure, to be confronted by it day in and day out. It is to live in a world whose standards of manliness are forever beyond one's reach, where one is continuously tested and challenged and continually found wanting. In self-defense, the husband retreats to the street corner. Here, where the measure of man is considerably smaller, and where weaknesses are somehow turned upside down and almost magically transformed into strengths, he can be, once again, a man among men.

Hypotheses 3 and 4: Race, Social Class and Parental Aspiration

Hypotheses 3 and 4 state that white parents and parents of the working- or middle-class are more likely than their black counterparts to urge their children to high achievement in school and eventually to a college education. The race hypothesis was drawn from the general literature concerning the way in which white-dominated school systems often alienate black students and their families (for example, U.S. Civil Rights Commission, 1967:78ff.; Kozol, 1967). Attached to the hypothesis was the caution that social class probably has a significant effect on the asserted relation—which necessitated examination of the joint influence of race and class upon parent's urging.

The appropriateness of caution is borne out in an ironic way by the data: while social class is positively though somewhat weakly related to parental aspiration (Somers' D = +.25***,) race shows no relation at all (D = .004). When both factors are considered simultaneously, however, a pattern emerges that is interesting because of its unexpected direction. Figure 8, which displays the relation between class and parental aspiration, reveals that the only substantial difference between the races is found among the lower-class parents. But contrary to the implication of the cautionary note, lower-class black students are somewhat *more* likely to report that their parents urge them to high educational achievement than are lower-class white students (24% to 15%). The same trend is observed in the working class, although the difference is smaller (36% to 30%). The association (Somers' D) of race with parental aspiration within the three class groupings is −.09 in the

Figure 8—Parental educational aspiration, according to race and social class.

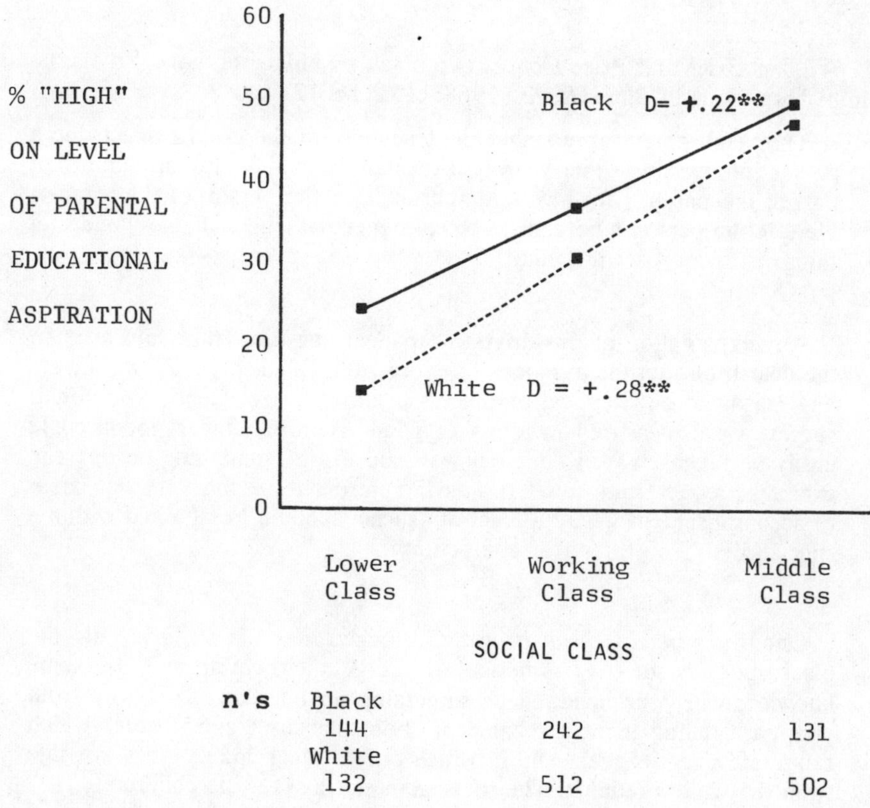

lower class, −.11* in the working class, and .004 in the middle class. While the black parents probably are discontent with the schools their children attend, they also probably see education as the only legitimate route to upward mobility (Bernard, 1966:135-137). Thus the data in Figure 8 may be used to infer that hypothesis 3 concerning race and parental aspiration is not only refuted, but is even slightly reversed: contrary to prediction, the black students report their parents as having higher educational aspirations than are reported of white parents.

The positive relationship between social class and parental aspiration predicted in hypothesis 4 is discovered in the data of Figure 8, but its strength is not great (D = +.22*** for black parents and +.28*** for whites). In either race, the middle-class students are about twice as likely as those of the lower class to state that their parents strongly urge them toward high educational attainment.

This positive but moderate relation of social class to the concern of parents and students for education, together with the fact that blacks report higher educational orientation than whites of the same class is demonstrated consistently throughout these data. (Coleman *et al.,* 1966:278-280). The pattern calls into serious question the assumption that blacks of low income are especially likely to ignore or reject actively the ideal of educational achievement. The reality of educational opportunity is, of course, quite another matter.

William Grier and Price Cobbs, two black psychiatrists, have put the issue into sharp focus in *Black Rage* (1968:115, 116, 128):

> The black parent approaches the teacher with the great respect due a person of learning. The soaring expectations which are an important part of the parent's feelings find substance in the person of the teacher. Here is the person who can do for this precious child all the wonderful things a loving parent cannot.
>
> * * *
>
> Any explanation of this drive toward learning must take into account the dearth of alternative modes of expression. Black people have always had reason to be skeptical of success in other fields of endeavor, for, if success were measured in terms of goods acquired, those goods could easily be taken away. Education was said to be "something no one can ever take away from you." It was therefore one of the very few areas of accomplishment where a level of "success" could be attained within a special Jim Crow arena of competition.
>
> * * *
>
> Our thesis is that black people are locked in a life struggle, and the black mothers all over America who urge their children: "Get some knowledge in your head; that's something no one can take away from you," are telling them a great deal about a vicious social order which rapes and exploits them and in which only a black man's ideas are safe from the white predator. The message is not lost on the children.

Hypotheses 5 and 6: Race, Social Class and Measured Verbal Ability

A wide range of literature documents hypothesis 5, that white students receive higher scores on measures of verbal ability than do black students. For examples, see Deutsch (1964), the wide range of research reviewed by Pettigrew (1964:111-135) and of course Jensen's controversial article (1968b). An even more extensive literature supports hypothesis 6's assertion of a direct relationship between measured verbal ability and social class (Deutsch, 1965; Pavenstedt, 1965; Jensen, 1968a; Whiteman and Deutsch, 1968).

The Coleman report (1966) itself shows strikingly that the average black child starts school about one and one-half years below the average white child in measured verbal ability, and thereafter drops steadily behind. By the age of twelve, the black child is over three years behind (*ibid.*, p. 273). Yet it is relatively rare that both race and social class are considered simultaneously in the analysis of any form of mental capacity. In the data of this study, the correlations of measured verbal ability with race (r = +.43**) and with social class (r = .25** for blacks, .43** for whites) are quite substantial. But the degree to which these are separate rather than overlapping relations can be seen only in joint-effect plots such as that contained in Figure 9.

The white students much more frequently score in the top half of the range of verbal ability by percentage ratios of 2.3:1 in the lower class, 2.1:1 in the working class, and an unusually large 2.6:1 in the middle class. The additive nature of the effects of race and class on measured verbal ability perhaps can be grasped more clearly by seeing that a middle-class white student is over 8 times as likely to be in the high half on measured verbal ability as is a lower-class black student (.81/.10 = 8.1:1).

As social class rises, race is more strongly related to the score on the verbal ability measure: D = +.13** for lower-class students, +.30** for working-class students, and +.50*** among middle-class students. Since developed ability is in large part a product of cognitive richness of the environment, this pattern may be interpreted as indicating that a middle-class economic position still does not provide blacks with the networks of communication that encourage development of these capacities.

Viewing it as a problem of determining the relationship between social class and measured verbal ability and controlling race, we find that both relations are positive, but much stronger among whites: +.13*** for blacks as compared to +.30*** for whites.

These patterns give strong support to both hypotheses 5 and 6 but also suggest that the lower-class situation may be more stultifying to whites than to blacks, relative to their higher-class counterparts, while to blacks the "benefits" of the middle-class condition may not be so powerful as to whites. Many more factors than simply economics are at work.

Figure 9—Measured verbal ability according to race and social class.

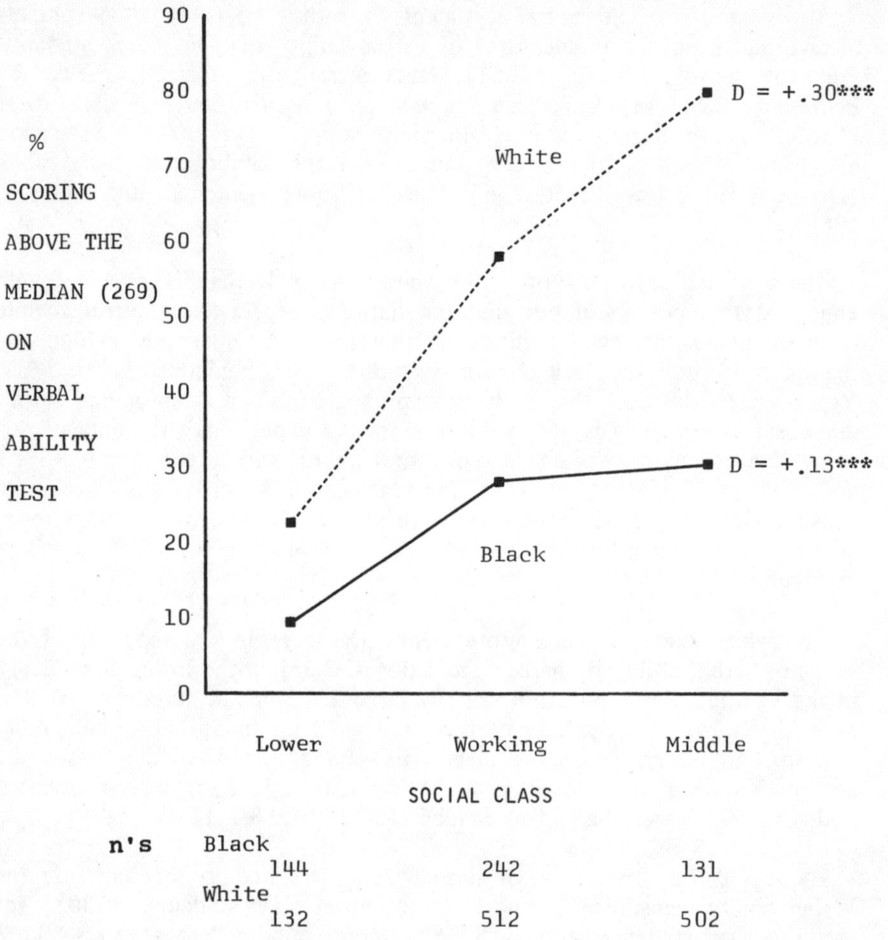

Hypotheses 7 and 8: Race, Social Class and Self-Conception

Race—Self-hatred in members of minorities has been a consistent theme of social-psychological writing. Thus marginality, self-alienation, self-consciousness and self-disparagement are interpreted as essential features of Jewishness in a largely Gentile world (Stonequist, 1937; Lewin, 1948, esp. ch. 12; and Seeman, 1959). More recently, the focus of attention has shifted to the situation of black people (cf. Kardiner and Ovesey, 1951; Pettigrew, 1964:6-11; Drake, 1965; Rainwater, 1966; esp. p. 187ff.; Silberman, 1964; and Proshansky and Newton, 1968). Whatever the substantive focus, the asserted relation is the same: a member of a social category, disparaged and discriminated against, is likely to internalize the meanings clinging to the stereotypes of it and to the realities of the treatment he is given, and thus come to conceive of himself in similarly disparaging cognitive and evaluative terms. Proshansky and Newton (1968) put the argument elegantly:

> Underlying our discussion of the Negro's self-concept is the reality of the discriminatory social caste-system in America with its historic origins in the institution of slavery. We see this system as imposing a double burden on the Negro through severe social and economic inequalities and through the heavy psychological consequences suffered by the Negro who is forced to play an inferior role. There are obvious differences in schools, housing, employment, and income; less visible, but equally serious, are the heavy psychological costs of low self-esteem, feelings of helplessness, and basic identity conflict. (pp. 178-179)
>
> * * *
>
> The Negro child is eventually forced to acknowledge and accept his Negro identity; this acceptance of his race may decrease but it does not eliminate the fundamental conflict involved in the development of his self-identity. What he is and can ever hope to be, as a Negro, is somewhat less than what he would be, or could ever hope to be, if he were white. The child's awareness of this conflict may be conscious or unconscious; however; the conflict itself tends to nourish feelings of self-doubt and a sense of inadequacy, if not actual self-hatred. Given these circumstances, we would expect the Negro child not only to be "sensitive" to the question of "who he is," but also to characterize himself in unfavorable terms, that is, to reveal a negative self-image. (p. 191)

There are strong indications that self-categorization in racial terms is learned as early as the age of three, and that these identifications are likely to carry negative valence (see, for example, Clark and Clark, 1947; Goodman, 1952; and the many studies reviewed by Proshansky and Newton, 1968: esp. pp. 186-196).

Yet other research suggests that members of rejected minorities may score quite high on direct measures of self-evaluation. For example, I found that the black and the Jewish junior-college students scored higher on a self-esteem scale than did non-Jewish whites, Mexican-Americans or Orientals (Gordon, 1963:151-153). Similarly, Rosenberg found that Jewish students scored higher in self-esteem than any other ethnic group in a very well-conducted study of some 5,000 high school juniors and seniors (1965:50-59).

A variety of explanations might be offered of relatively high scores on self-evaluation among teenaged members of disparaged minorities. Perhaps, as Rosenberg argues, strong ethnic neighborhood and interpersonal support may have helped these young people to overcome early negative learning. Secondly, it may be that research on the unfavorable aspects of identity among Negroes and Jews has been over-focused on adults who have already repeatedly experienced personal exclusion or trauma due to ethnic prejudice, something that young teenagers still in a relatively protected and homogeneous school environment may have yet to learn. Third, students of any age who are still in school may entertain a more favorable self-conception than those who have dropped out. Since the drop-out rate is likely to be substantially higher among blacks, it is probable that those who remain enjoy an even more favorable self-conception than is the case with others. Fourth, there is without question a tendency toward a compensatory or false-positive stand on questions dealing directly with self-evaluation among persons who have strong reasons to feel negatively toward themselves. I refer here to a specifically ethnic sensitivity (over and above an idiosyncratic component of personality, the motivation to attain social desirability), that often blocks the expression or even the awareness of negative self-referential meanings (Wylie, 1961; Crowne and Marlowe, 1964; Gordon, 1968a; 1968b). This problem can be approached only through very careful use of screening devices, studies of criterion-validity employing other types of measures, and construct-validity estimations involving interrelations of measures of self-conception with other variables about which we have some theoretical ideas or empirical experience.

In any case, since the ninth-graders in our sample are relatively young and since statistics on them are not yet strongly skewed by dropping out, we predict in hypothesis 7 that black students have *less* favorable self-conceptions across all the measured aspects than do white.

Social class—Here our hypothesis can be grounded in a much more straightforward manner. A persistent theme in social-psychological research on stratification has highlighted pervasive elements of negative self-conception among lower- and working-class persons, especially in adolescence (cf. Davis, Gardner and Gardner, 1941; Hollingshead, 1949; and Rosenberg, 1965: 39-41). On the same symbolic-interactionist assumption that a person's conception of himself tends to reflect (among other things) the way he is treated by his significant others, hypothesis 8 is that social class is directly related to favorability of self-conception across all dimensions.

Figure 10B reveals that the positive relation (predicted in hypothesis 8) between social class and favorability of self-conception is supported as to direction across all six dimensions, but with quite small degrees of association (Somers' D's from the original tables ranging from +.07** with basic self-acceptance to +.18*** with global self-esteem and up to .20*** with self-rated brightness). It should also be remembered that the index of over-all competence is actually constructed from the measure of academic competence as well as other items, and that the measure of global self-esteem draws upon all the others. Thus it must be concluded that social class is positively but weakly related to favorability of self-conception.

Comparison of these data with those in Figure 10A leads us to infer that the favorability of self-conception is even more weakly related to race. Although the findings are in the predicted direction in five out of six non-independent comparisons, the magnitudes of these relations are very near zero in all but two cases. On the indices of self-rated brightness, self-determination and global self-esteem the black students score appreciably lower than do the whites (D's = .14***, +.15*** and +.10***). However, self-determination is of central theoretical importance, whether viewed from the perspective of fate control (Coleman, 1966:288-289), powerlessness

Figure 10—Relations of race and social class to favorability of self-conceptions.

10A: Self-Conceptions by Race (minimum base n's)	Black (431)	White (1096)	Somers' D and Chi-Square probability level: *=<.05 **=≤01 ***=≤001 for entire table
1. Basic self-acceptance "If I could change, I would be someone different from myself." % agreeing (rejecting self)	% 28	% 22	+.07*
2. "How bright do you think you are in comparison with the other students in your grade?" % saying above average or among the brightest	36	44	+.14***
3. Academic competence index % in upper quarter	22	26	+.02
4. Over-all competence index % "high"	11.4	11.2	-.007
5. Self-determination index % "high"	17	28	+.15***
6. Global self-esteem index % "high"	19	28	+.10***

10B: Self-Conceptions by Social Class (minimum base n's)	Lower (217)	Working (692)	Middle (599)	
1. Basic self-acceptance (as above), % rejecting self	% 33	% 24	% 20	+.07**
2. Self-perceived relative brightness % saying above average or among the brightest	28	38	50	+.20***
3. Academic competence index % in upper quarter	14	22	32	+.16***
4. Over-all competence index % "high"	8	9	15	+.10***
5. Self-determination index % "high"	20	21	31	+.13***
6. Global self-esteem index % "high"	12	23	33	+.18***

(Seeman, 1959; Drake, 1965), internal vs. external control (Rotter, 1966), or the sense of personal autonomy (Douvan and Adelson, 1966: 130ff.; and Gordon, 1968c).

Figure 11 depicts the way in which social class is related to sensed self-determination within the two racial groups. The first conclusion is that black students fall clearly below white students in each social class (the D's on the full tables are +.10 for lower class, +.08 for working class, and +.22*** for middle class). Second, self-determination is not appreciably related to social class among blacks, and among whites shows only a marked difference in the middle class, where high sensed self-determination is most frequently found.

Recent writings based on much more vital and immediately meaningful data provide abundant support for the conclusion that blacks tend to feel low in self-determination:

> As boys approach adulthood, masculinity becomes more and more bound up with money making. In a capitalistic society economic wealth is inextricably interwoven with manhood. Closely allied is power—power to control and direct other men, power to influence the course of one's own and other lives. The more lives one can influence, the greater the power. The ultimate power is the freedom to understand and alter one's life. It is this power, both individually and collectively, which has been denied the black man (Grier and Cobbs, 1968:50).

> As for the future, the young street-corner man has a fairly good picture of it. . . . It is a future in which everything is uncertain except the ultimate destruction of his hopes and the eventual realization of his fears. The most he can reasonably look forward to is that these things do not come too soon. Thus, when Richard squanders a week's pay in two days it is not because, like an animal or a child, he is "present-time oriented," unaware of the future and the hopelessness of it all (Liebow, 1966:66).

Figure 11—Sensed self-determination according to social class and race.

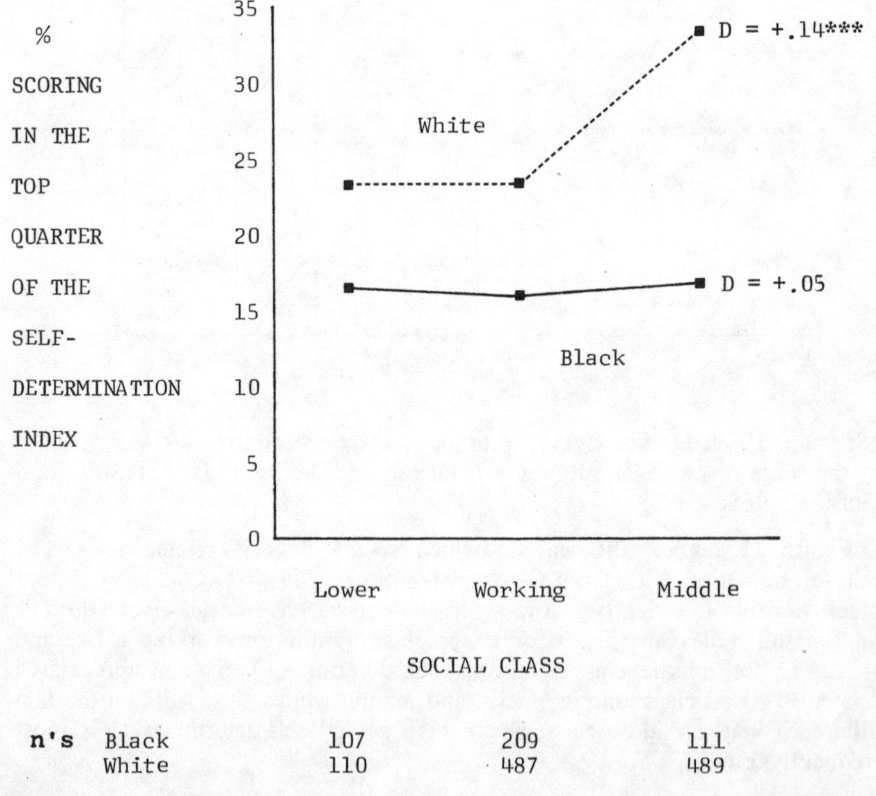

n's		Lower	Working	Middle
	Black	107	209	111
	White	110	487	489

Some interesting joint relations of race and social class to global self-esteem may be seen in Figure 12. These data portray more graphically the positive relation between social class and self-esteem within each race (+.17** black; +.16*** white). That these relations are meaningful can be inferred from the fact that a middle-class white student is almost three times as likely to score high on self-esteem as is his lower-class counterpart (34.1% to 11.6%). Similarly, a middle-class black student is over twice as likely to score high as is a lower-class black student.

Secondly, Figure 12 shows that the sharp jump in the percentage scoring high in self-esteem comes between working class and middle class among blacks, while the whites' slope of the curve is more even. The slight over-all difference in scores on self-esteem between the races is most pronounced among the working-class students (26% of the whites scoring high, as against 17% of the blacks; D = +.08*), is smaller in the middle class (34% to 30%; D = +.05) and disappears in the lower class (12% of whites scoring high as against 13% of blacks; D = +.02).

Third, Figure 12 provides another way of showing that, in this population, social class is a more important determinant of self-esteem than is race—a middle-class black student is 2.6 times as likely to score high on self-esteem

Figure 12—Joint relation of race and social class to global self-esteem.

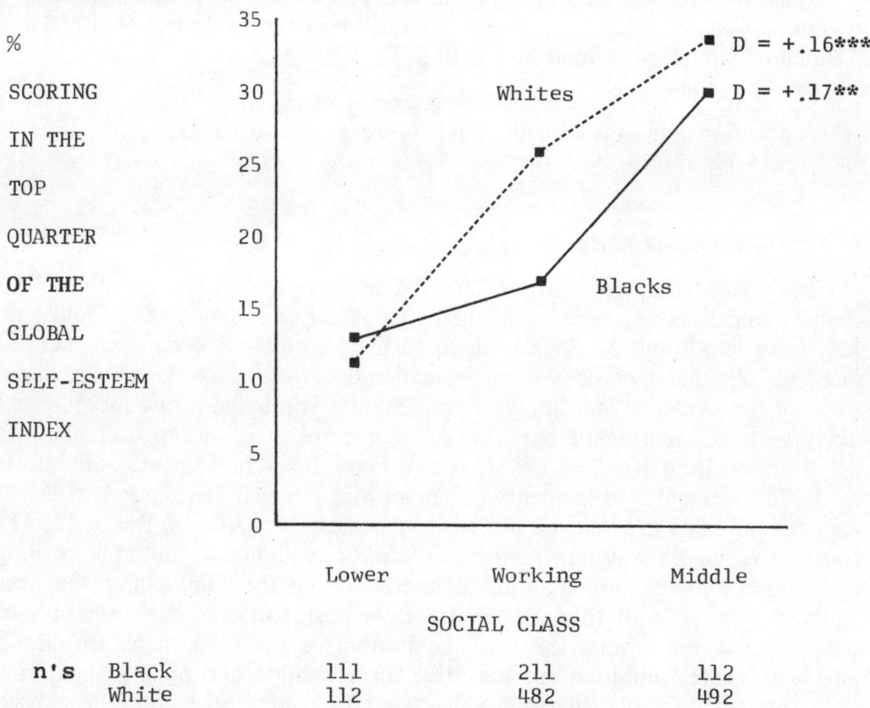

than is a lower-class white student. The autobiographies of black writers clearly convey the point regarding race:

> I am an invisible man. . . . I am invisible, understand, simply because people refuse to see me. . . . When they approach me they see only my surroundings, themselves, or figments of their imagination—indeed, everything and anything except me (Ellison, 1947:7).

> "One day, you'll probably understand . . . when the dog in you starts comin' out."
> I'd say, "What dog in me, Mama?"
> "Every man's got a little bitta dog in him. Your daddy got a whole lotta dog in him too."
> "Yeah, well, I sure hope I ain't got no dog in me, Mama."
> I didn't understand that dog thing, not right then anyway. Then one day I heard a girl say, "A nigger is nothing but a dog." And I remembered Mama telling me, "Boy, don't be so doggish," when I would bring home one girl one day and another girl the next. I got the meaning of the dog in the man. "Yeah, all men have a little dog in them," I repeated to my self (Brown, 1965:383).

Regarding class, Liebow's statement may be taken as a paradigm of the plight of lower-class men of whatever race:

> However far he has gone in school, he is illiterate or almost so; however many jobs he has had or hard he has worked, he is essentially unskilled. Armed with models who have failed, convinced of his own worthlessness, illiterate and unskilled, he enters marriage and the job market with the smell of failure all around him (1966:211).

This complex web connecting race, social class, and various aspects of self-conception must be kept in mind as we go on to consider the effect of each on aspiration.

Hypotheses 9 and 10: Race, Social Class and Aspiration

Class—Recent discussions of level of aspiration of black youths (Proshansky and Newton, 1968) and the economically disadvantaged (Goldstein, 1967, esp. ch. 2 and 3) have brought to light a number of apparent contradictions. Whether the focus is on educational or on occupational aspiration, some of the evidence and analyses suggest that youths with low incomes are likely to be despairing of any chance of occupational success, reluctant to delay gratification when to do so is necessary for achievement, and hostile to the institutional arrangements of school and job that (in theory, at least) facilitate mobility. In one of the earliest discussions, Allison Davis (1941) stated that the class system restricts children's symbolic worlds and learning environments by confining intimate interaction in the family and the peer clique to the circle of those of similar class position, while the pressures of subsistence living among those at the bottom of the class structure simultaneously make "ambition" or the drive for education and high occupational skills an unattainable luxury. This "vicious circle" viewpoint has been perceptively advocated also by Genevieve Knupfer (1947), who proposed that lack of confidence in the cultural thought life of the community leads to low levels of societal participation, to attitudes of submissiveness and to the expectation of failure, all of which combine to assure that what economic opportunities are available are missed. Hollingshead's Elmtown Study (1949) provided some of the first data in support of the theory of the cycle of poverty, and many more recent pieces of research have borne out the general argument (especially Empey, 1956; Sewell, Haller, and Strauss, 1957; Stephenson, 1957; and Elder, 1962b).

Yet there are also indications that social class may be related more strongly to the anticipations that are most closely bound to the means actually available to the student than it is to those fantasies or preferences regarding the world of work that the common culture, especially the mass media, defines as desirable. Robert Merton has elaborated this reasoning (1957, especially pp. 136-139), and it has received empirical support in the work of Turner (1964) and also in the studies by Empey (1956) and Stephenson (1957), both of whom distinguished between ideal preferences and actual intentions, and conceptualized the gap between them.

On the basis of this rather extensive body of evidence, hypothesis 10 is that social class is directly related to both educational aspiration and occupational expectation. However, an attempt will be made where appropriate to take account of several sub-issues such as the "reality level" of the aspirations (ideal, intent, plan, expectation, concrete action already in progress, etc.), and also of the certainty or firmness of those indications.

Race and aspiration—Studies of the aspirations of black young people are rare, and much of the work that does exist yields seemingly contradictory conclusions. While impressionistic materials generally portray widespread despair, apathy and hostility (cf. Drake, 1965; Brown, 1965; Rainwater, 1966; Kozol, 1967), social class is often so confounded with race as to make inference very difficult (see the studies reviewed by Goldstein, 1967: 69-72; and Proshansky and Newton, 1968:196-202).

More elaborate studies, such as those by Stephenson (1957) and by Rosen (1959) indicate that the blacks' levels of general motivation to achieve, academic drive, educational aspiration, and occupational preference may be as high or even higher than the whites' of the same social class level—and this despite the fact that there is less tangible return to Negroes on their investment in education than there is to whites (Blau and Duncan, 1967: ch. 6).

An important deduction from this literature is that lower- and working-class black young people are likely to entertain even higher fantasy ideals than whites, but also that there is likely to be a larger gap between their ideal preferences and their actual expectations. Reduced expectations seem to match better the opportunity structures the blacks face, and are likely to reflect their less sheltered environment.

Hypothesis 9 expresses this principle of differing realism in the perception of opportunity: black students have higher educational desires but lower occupational expectations than do white students and blacks; moreover, are less likely to have actually penetrated channels of academic mobility by being enrolled in a college preparatory program and by accumulating the kind of grade record necessary for admission to college.

The data in Figure 13 lead to the conclusion that both hypotheses 9 and 10 are supported. Even before race is controlled, they provide evidence of clear although moderate positive relationships between social class and aspiration, whether the latter be expressed as the desire to be one of the best students in the class (D = +.09***), as the amount of education desired (+.26***) or as occupational expectation (+.25***). Simultaneous consideration of race sharpens the focus. The most striking instance of the class relation is found in Figure 13B, where a middle-class white is shown to be about 2.8 times as likely to indicate a desire for a B.A. or advanced degree as is a lower-class white. Even the smallest class difference—that between the percentage of working and middle-class blacks desiring advanced education (51% to 60%)—is substantial. Furthermore, all the relations between class and aspiration are somewhat weaker in the case of black students. This finding lends further support to the previous interpretation concerning the flattened impact of class within the black caste.

A smaller but still meaningful set of differences supports hypothesis 9: the black students more frequently report a desire to be among the best students in their classes and to obtain advanced education. As to how good a student the respondent wants to be, the values of Somers' D for the relations with race of the three class groups are —.17**, —.16***, and —.10. The relation of race to educational desire is —.10 in the lower-class students, —.05 in the working-class, and+.04 in the middle-class. Thus the hypothesis that blacks report higher educational aspirations than whites is supported in 5 of the 6 race-and-class comparisons, failing only in the case of the slight (4%) reversal in the middle-class desire to go to college or graduate school.

Regarding occupational expectation, the data in Figure 13C support hypothesis 9 only in the middle-class comparison: the black students are substantially *less* likely to say that they actually expect to become high-ranking professionals—managers, owners, or executives (D = +.16**). Lower- and working-class students did not differ appreciably (D = +.03, +.05*) by race in the frequency with which they stated that they expected to enter one of the higher occupations. These students are still quite young (most of them being 14 years old), and it may be that only the middle-class blacks have as yet been exposed to the difficulties faced by older brothers and sisters or friends in trying to get through college and gain entrance to an occupation which enjoys high status. If this is the case, we can expect that working- and lower-class blacks as well will soon begin to grow aware of the gap between ideal preference and actual expectation.

Further clarification of the relations between race, social class, and orientation toward education may be found in the data of Figure 14. Although the black students were much more likely than the whites of the same social class to say that they wanted to be among the best students, Figure 14A shows that their self-reported grade averages for the previous year were well below

Figure 13—Aspirations according to race and social class.

13A—"How good a student do you want to be in school?"

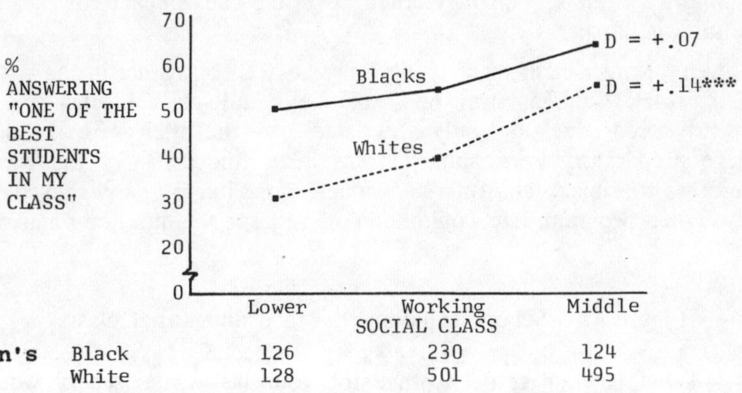

13B—"How far do you want to go in school?"

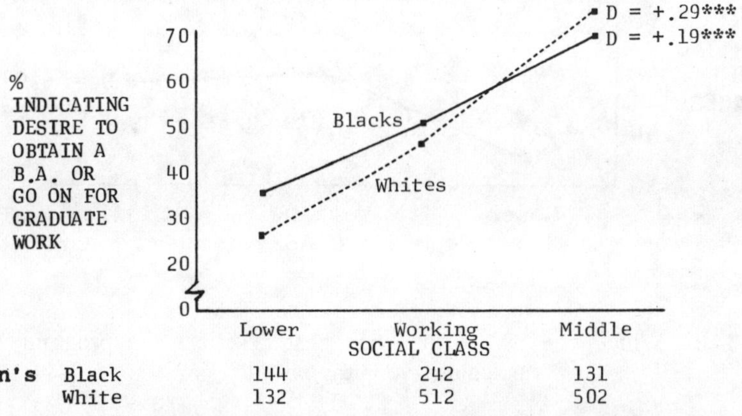

13C—"When you finish your education, what sort of a job do you think you will have?"

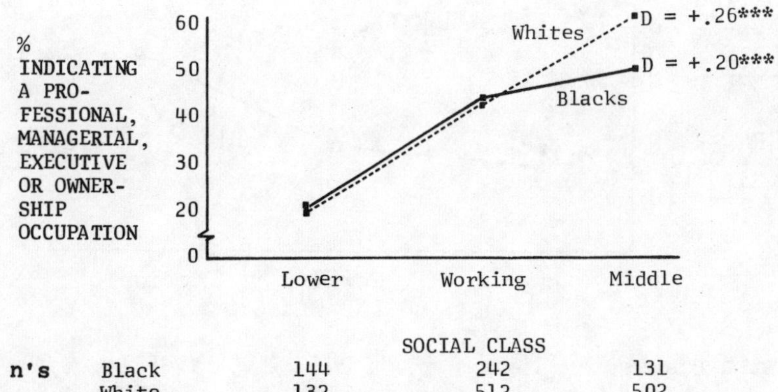

those of the whites, especially in the middle class (D = +.22***). One possible interpretation of this large difference (71% to 50% reporting grades of A or B) is that the middle-class blacks are more likely to be part of a small minority in the schools they attend, with the consequence that academic competition is harsher.

An even stronger element of reality may be seen operating in the patterns of Figure 14B. Whereas over 65% of the middle-class blacks said they wanted advanced education, only 35% said even that they were enrolled in a college preparatory curriculum (versus 72% and 53% of the whites). Furthermore, the black students were much more likely to say they did not know yet what program they would be in, or to leave the question unanswered

Figure 14—School situation, by race and social class.

14A—What is your grade average for your last year's school work?

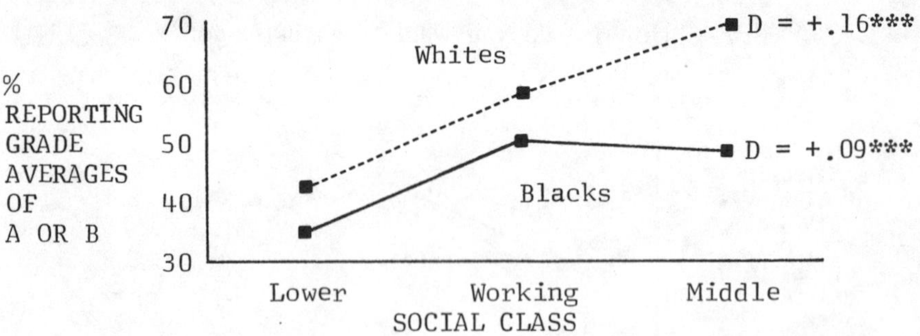

14B—Which one of the following best describes the program or curriculum you are enrolled in?

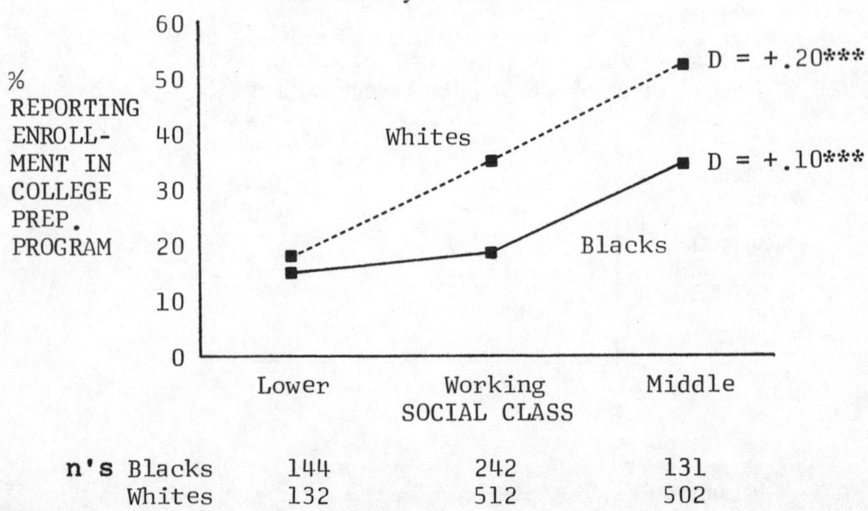

(41, 26, and 30 percent of the black class groups as against 33, 16 and 14 percent of the white class groups).

As was the case of educational and occupational aspiration, social class is less strongly related to achievement in the black students. In addition, a new pattern becomes evident among them: unrealistic mobilizing of the effective but difficult means of attaining the idealized goals.

Elliot Liebow has specified some of the ways in which lower-class men (especially blacks, although the pattern seems to be quite general) are likely to deal with the world of work:

> Convinced of their inadequacies, not only do they not seek out those few better-paying jobs which test their resources, but they actively avoid them, gravitating in a mass to the menial, routine jobs which offer no challenge—and therefore pose no threat—to the already diminished images they have of themselves (1966:54).

FAMILY STRUCTURE AS PREDICTIVE OF PARENTAL ASPIRATION, MEASURED VERBAL ABILITY, AND SELF-CONCEPTIONS

One of the virtues of theoretical causal models or path diagrams such as that given in Figure 1 is that they make possible formulation of hypotheses concerning the relationship of intervening variables to an outcome, apart from the effect of independent variables that may be shaping both. Thus hypotheses 11, 12, and 13 concern the relationship of the structure of family economic roles to the educational aspiration of the parents, measured verbal ability, and various aspects of self-conception, all independent of their mutual relations to race and social class.

Hypothesis 11: Parental Educational Aspiration and Family Structure

Study of qualitative differences in the social relationships between parents and children in families of different role configurations is beginning to make some progress (see for example, Elder, 1962, 1963; Pavenstedt, 1965; Goldstein, 1967:ch. 1). For the most part, however, they do not include educational aspiration and urging in the context of the interaction that is being analyzed. In the present data, the various categories of the structure of family roles do show significant differences and a roughly linear relation to the level of parental educational aspiration (D = +.24***). However, hypothesis 11 requires us to make sure that these differences are not simply spurious reflections of the fact that the differently structured families also differ in race and social class. Figure 15 gives the percentage of cases in each family configuration which scored in the *lower* third, with the students in each social class and race plotted separately. The lower third was chosen as a way of maximizing the validity of the students' reports about their parents' urging, since it can be plausibly assumed that few of the students will have made their way by intentional deceit into the lower third of the scores on parental aspirations for their offsprings' education.

Although the patterns are somewhat complex and the number of cases on which percentages are calculated are too often much smaller than one would desire, it is apparent that large differences in parental aspiration among families varying in role configuration remain, even after social class and race have been controlled. First, the general trend of the relations is in the predicted direction in every one of the six race-and-class comparisons. The magnitudes of these relations are not at all strong, ranging from D = +.05

Figure 15—Parental educational aspiration in the various configurations of family role structure, by class and race.

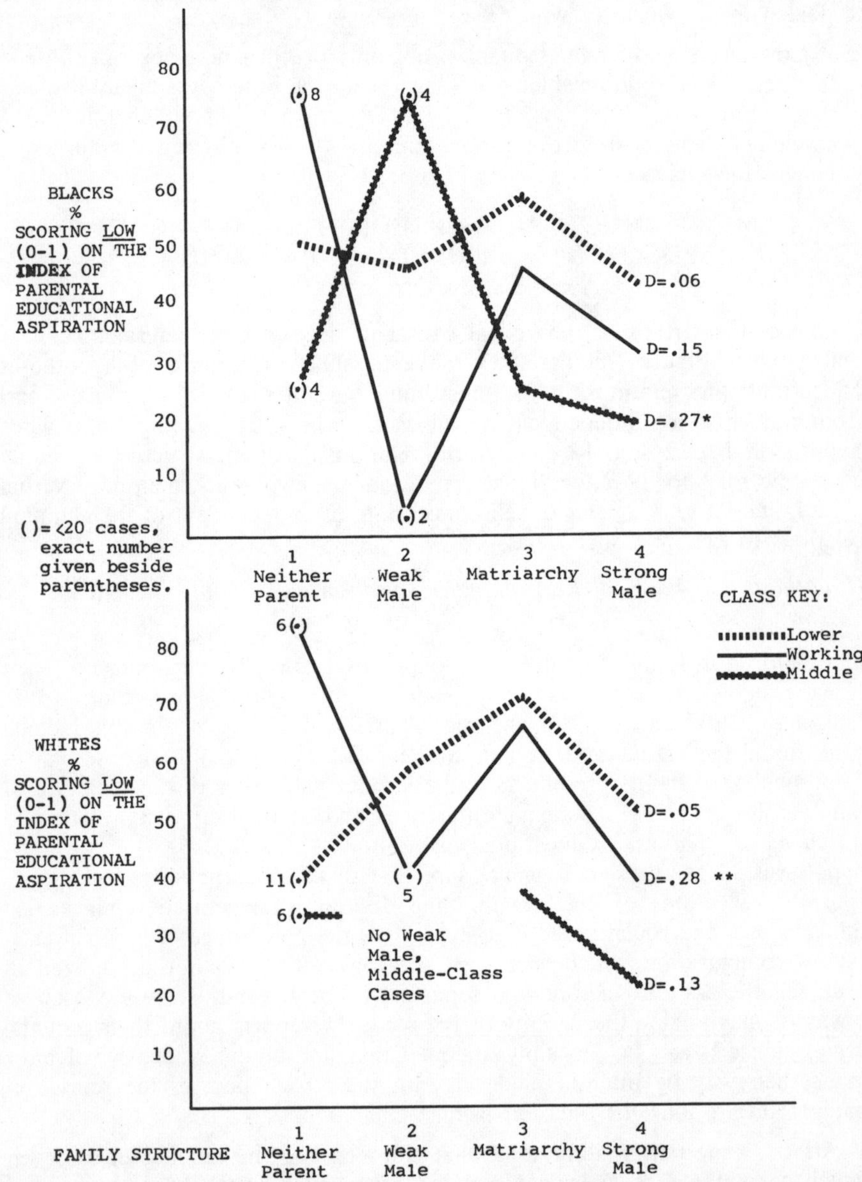

among lower-class whites to +.28** among working-class whites. Among blacks, the relation is also weakest in the lower class (+.06), but highest in the middle class (+.27*).

In all instances where there are enough cases to make meaningful comparisons, the cultural ideal (#4, the "strong-male" father figure is present and providing the family's main support) shows the lowest proportion of students scoring in the lower third of the index of parental aspiration. Furthermore, the "strong-male" configuration is in every case distinctly rarer in this proportion than is the matriarchy (#3). It should be noted, however, that this outcome is made likely (though not strictly entailed) by the way in which the index of parental aspiration was constructed; that is, one point was added for each report of a parent desiring the student to do especially well in school or to complete at least a B.A. Such aspirations were counted even if the parent expressing the desire was reported as not currently living in the student's home, but students lacking any father or mother figure will naturally score low on this index.

Comparison of the "weak-male" configuration (#2) with the matriarchy (#3) reveals that in 4 out of the 6 pairings, the matriarchy has an appreciably greater proportion of students who fall in the lower third of the scores on parental aspiration. Only among middle-class black students does the "weak-male" configuration have a higher proportion than does the matriarchy. The percentages among these students and working-class blacks and whites should not be taken as even roughly reliable, since they are based on unacceptably low numbers of respondents (4, 2, and 5, respectively). Where the number of cases is large enough to permit comparison (only among the lower-class blacks and whites), the "weak-male" configuration shows about the same proportion who score low on parents' educational aspiration as does the "strong-male" category, both being distinctly lower proportions than are found in the matriarchal arrangment.

Finally, the "neither-parent-present" category (#1) shows a relatively high proportion of students who fall in the lower third as to the parental aspiration index, although equalled or exceeded by the matriarchy in 4 of the 6 comparisons. Only in the working-class groups (both black and white) does this type of household outdo the matriarchy in the proportion scoring low on parental aspiration, and these two sub-groups are very small (8 and 6 cases). Perhaps the alteration in the patterns suggested, though most tenuously, by these few cases, can be explained in terms of the working-class mothers' desire for their children to assume the role of provider as soon as possible, since no welfare money would be lost with the increased family income, as might well be the case among the lower-class families.

From the entire pattern of interrelations it is possible to conclude that, as predicted in hypothesis 11, the structure of family economic roles (as formulated here in terms of an ordered set of categories approximating in different degree the cultural ideal of an intact family in which the father is the main breadwinner) is related positively, although weakly, to the level of reported parents' aspiration for students' education, even after class and race are controlled.

Hypothesis 12: Family Structure and Verbal Ability

The diversity and richness of the verbal interaction experienced by children in their formative years may be expected to affect their acquisition of verbal skills (Brofenbrenner, 1958; Deutsch, 1965; Pavenstedt, 1965; and the studies surveyed by Goldstein 1967:8-24). Since we are seeking an effect of family structure per se rather than of social class or ethnic subculture, we must try to isolate the specifically compositional or structural effects, as Inkeles (1968) and Smith (1968) have recently suggested. First, the complete family should provide a multiplicity of cognitive models and opportunities for interaction. Second, it may be plausibly assumed that any psychic damage brought on by a sense of parental rejection after a divorce or a separation hinders the child's general cognitive development through deep anxiety or cynical bitterness. Thus hypothesis 12 is that the family's structure of economic roles is associated with the student's score on the test of verbal ability, even after effects of race and social class have been taken into account.

The data of the present study give reasonable support to the hypothesis. An over-all F-test of the differences between the 4 family structures in their mean scores on verbal ability ($F = 46.1$, $df = 3$, and 1680, $p < .001$) shows very substantial differences. More easily visualized is the cross-tabular relation of family structure to the dichotomized verbal ability score (D = +.28***). This relation persists although in weakened form when race is controlled (+.10* for blacks, +.25*** for whites), or social class (D = +.07, +.10 and +.28*** for lower, working and middle class). Since our hypothesis requires separation of racial and social class factors from the relation of family structure and verbal ability, the data in Figure 16 have been arranged to facilitate the necessary comparisons.

The patterns of the white students are most clear. In addition to the previously demonstrated findings that the white students are much more likely to score high on verbal ability and that the three classes stand in perfect positive relation without overlap, the data on the white students in Figure 16 show a roughly linear positive relation between family structure and measured verbal ability. Within each social class, the configurations of the "strong-male" and the matriarchy stand equal to each other in the proportion of students scoring in the high half on verbal ability and much higher than the corresponding "neither-parent-present" case. Where cases in the "weak-male" situation exist (among the working- and lower-class whites), the proportion of verbally skilled students is much lower than in the corresponding matriarchy and "strong-male" arrangements, but appreciably higher than where the student lives with no father or mother figure. None of these relations is at all strong (D = +.11, +.06, and +.02 among lower-, working- and middle-class students), but the discrepancy between the "strong-male" and the matriarchy patterns, on the one hand, and the "weak-male" and "neither-parent-present," on the other, is sufficiently marked to warrant further attention.

Among the black students, social class does not make so consistent a difference in determining the level of verbal ability, and even in the most favorable situation (middle-class, with a strong father figure present) only

Figure 16—Verbal ability as related to family role structure after taking account of race and social class.

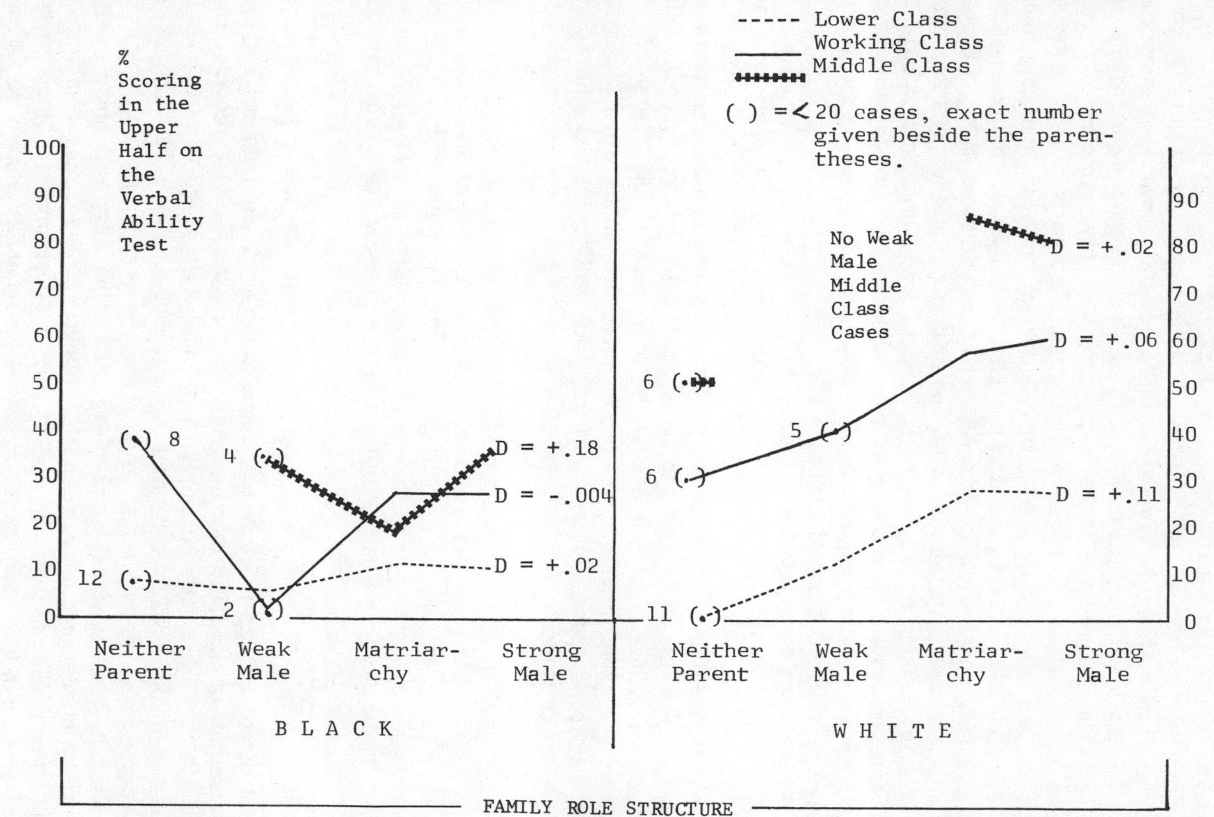

about 36% of the students scored in the upper half of the distribution. This middle-class black group is also unusual in that only in it does the matriarchy configuration contain a smaller proportion of verbally able students than does the "strong-male" category (19% to 36%; D = +.18 for the entire table). The "weak-male" configuration among the black students shows a slightly lower proportion of able students than does the matriarchy in the only group with a substantial number of cases (the lower-class group)—a proportion even slightly lower than is found among the "neither-parent-present" groups. The very small number of cases in the latter category precludes solid inferences, but possibly the "neither-parent-present" arrangement is associated with low verbal ability in middle-class students, but with markedly higher levels among the working-class students. That these least advantaged working-class students and the few lower-class students should score as high or higher than their counterparts who live with one or both parents suggests that young adolescents taken in as additional members of already large families or placed in institutions with large numbers of other children get more cognitive stimulation and verbal interaction than do children of the "non-verbal families" described by Jessie Bernard (1966:143ff).

The over-all patterns in Figure 16 present the culturally ideal form, two parents and a working father, as consistently associated with high proportions of high scorers on the verbal ability test. The matriarchal configuration is about equal to the both-parents situation in all cases but that of middle-class blacks, where it has only about half the proportion of high scorers. It may well be that these middle-class mothers' more demanding work role means that they spend appreciably less time with their children than do the working and lower class mothers.

The "weak-male" configuration is associated with lower scores on ability than the matriarchy or "strong-male" forms in four of the five comparisons in appropriate race-and-class settings, and the exception is based on only four cases. Although some of the relevant percentages are calculated on very small bases, the pattern is so consistent that it must be given some credence.

One interesting interpretation might be that, as a role model, an unemployed father figure in the home exerts two kinds of negative effect. On the level of content, he is likely to be less verbally skilled than his employed counterpart of the same race and class, and consequently to provide less in the way of positive verbal example. As to the nature of the "prospective self" that the unemployed father provides, a boy is likely to feel anxious and uncertain about his own future, as he pictures it in his father's example, while a girl may grow anxious over her own future marriage and home environment. In either case, increased anxiety about the future may combine with embarrassment and shame caused by present conditions to block effective performance in tests such as the measure of verbal ability used in the Coleman Study. This finding and interpretation lends further support to the more general assertion that the presence of a weak or negative role model may have more detrimental consequences than does the classic case of the absent father (cf. Gordon and Shea, 1967).

Hypothesis 31: Family Role Structure and Self-Conception

In an attempt to reduce somewhat problems of the invalidity of very favorable self-descriptions, the following analysis of the relation of family structure to self-conception is presented in terms of the percentages of students who characterize themselves *negatively*. Negative responses (Wylie, 1961:82 and passim; Gordon, 1968c) have been found likely to be of higher validity as interpretations of the respondents' own reflexive thoughts than are very positive answers, which are often contaminated with errors traceable to the desire for social approval.

Hypothesis 13 is that family role configurations are associated with corresponding patterns of self-conception, independent of race and social class. In particular, it is expected that the "strong-male" configuration is *least* associated with negative self-conceptions; the matriarchal form produces intermediate levels; "the weak-male" configuration is most likely to be associated with unfavorable conceptions of self, as is also the "neither-parent-present" pattern. Furthermore, these patterns are expected to differ across the various aspects of self tapped in the Coleman Study.

The data in Figure 17 show that before race and social class are controlled, all six self-conceptions do relate to family structure in the predicted direction, although the magnitudes are not great. In order of association with the ordered categories of the family structure are self-rated brightness (D = +.18**), global self-esteem (+.12**), the sense of self-determination (.11**), academic competence (+.08) and basic self-acceptance (+.06). On the index of over-all competence (not plotted in Figure 17) only the general pattern holds (the proportion scoring "low" ranges from +.21 to +.39, D = +.06, p <.16). When considered as a problem of comparing the means of the four-family structures on the continuous versions of the indices of self-conception, all the F-tests prove to be significant beyond the p <.001 level, except in the case of over-all competence. Actually, the present method of reporting the degree of linear trend in terms of Somers' D underestimates the degree of relationship, because fully 70% of the sample fall in the complete-family-working-father category (#4). If the difference between proportions is taken as the technique of presentation, we see that global self-esteem is related to the weak-male vs. strong-male distinction at a magnitude of +.24. Alternatively, a student living with neither parent is 1.7 times as likely to score in the lower third on self-esteem as is a student living with his mother and working father.

The situation in which both parents are present and the father is working is associated with lower levels of self-disparagement in all the aspects of self-conception. Second in favorability in all but academic concept and self-determination is the matriarchal situation. As predicted in hypothesis 13, where the father is present but does not work, the various forms of negative self-conceptions are very frequent (column 2 in Figure 17). These data thus support a line of work going back to E. Wright Bakke's writing on families in the Depression (1940: esp. ch. 6-9). Also confirming hypothesis 13 is the fact that the matriarchal pattern yields low-intermediate levels of self-disparagement on all measures. On the index of global self-esteem, self-disparagement is found in 39% of students in the matriarchal family, as compared to 60% of those in the "weak-male" configuration. The "neither-parent-present" category exhibits the highest levels of self-disparagement on self-rated brightness and self-determination, and a high-intermediate level on the other conceptions of self.

While the data of Figure 17 provide substantial confirmation of hypothesis 13, both family structure and self-conception are so intricately related to race and social class that these factors must be taken into account before it can be concluded that in this study the hypothesis has been confirmed.

Before the introduction of any controls, the relationship between family

Figure 17—Self-conception dimensions and family role structure configuration.

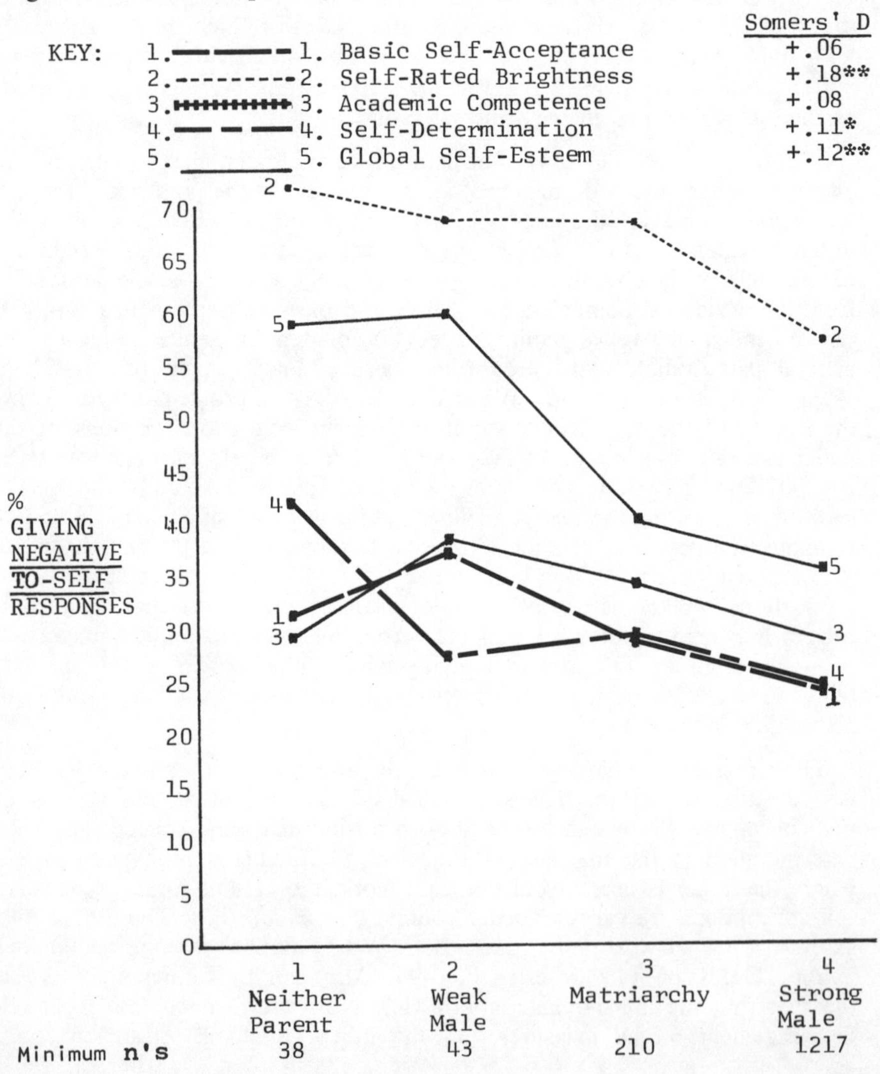

role structure and the trichotomized version of global self-esteem is +.12**. The same relation, after controlling race, is +.09 among whites and +.11 among blacks, indicating that race plays no appreciable role in conditioning the relationship. When social class is introduced as the control variable, the relations between family role structure and global self-esteem in the lower, working and middle class are found to measure +.02, +.03, and +.09,* respectively. Thus, social class is seen to have a greater conditioning effect than race. Further, close examination of the detailed tables shows some intricate effects on the family/self-conception relation depending upon particular combinations of race and class. Since hypothesis 13 concerns the forms of this relation independent of race and class, it is necessary to inspect the data of Figure 18 before a conclusion can be drawn.

The plotted points in Figure 18 show the percentage of students in each category of family structure who scored in the lower third on the index of global self-esteem, with separate indication of each social class within each race. While many of the race-and-class family categories contain so few cases that the calculated percentages are only very rough guides to what would be obtained if all of the urban Northeast ninth-graders living in a particular family situation were tested, the present analysis is concerned with general trends and patterns of consistency and difference between various sub-sections of the sample rather than with precise estimates of population

Figure 18—Family role structure and global self-esteem, by social class and race.

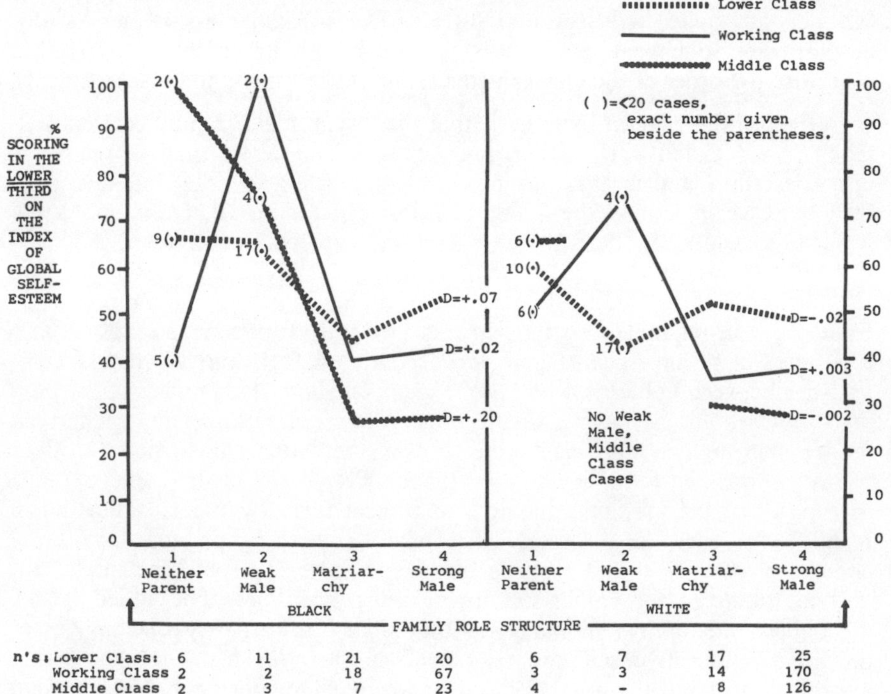

parameters. Also, interpretations can make use of the measures of association (Somers' D) that take into consideration all the cases in a table rather than just those who scored in the lower third and were therefore plotted in graphic displays such as Figure 18.

The left-hand portion of Figure 18 reveals that the black students' patterns continue to show low rates of self-disparagement in the "strong-male" and matriarchy configurations as compared with the "weak-male" and "neither-parent-present" forms. The overall relation of family structure to self-esteem remains positive but low, and is seen to be much stronger among middle-class black students (+.20) than among working- (+.02) and lower-class students (+.07). Among those in the "neither-parent-present" category, self-disparagement is very frequently found in the lower-class students (66%, but only 9 cases) and in both of the middle-class categories, but in only 2 of the 5 working-class respondents.

The data on the white students (plotted on the right side of Figure 18) show somewhat different variations on the same general themes. The complete families with working fathers again have low self-rejection rates, and again the matriarchies have almost equally low percentages. Where there is also a father who does not work, self-disparagement is lowest among the lower-class students and exceptionally high among the few from the working class (3/4). This last finding suggests that there is some truth in the argument that the norms of middle-class blacks (where self-rejection was found to be at precisely this high rate) are much the same as those of working-class whites. (Bernard, 1967: esp. Ch. 2). As was the case with lower-class black students living apart from both parents, rejection rates of lower-class whites in this situation are quite high (around 60%). The working-class whites of this category are somewhat less likely to score in the lower third (3/6), but otherwise the order of the classes is the same as it is among the black students.

In light of the general hypothesis that the "weak-male" family role constellation is associated with higher rates of self-denigration than is the more often described matriarchal situation, it is interesting to note that this is, in fact, the case in four of the five comparisons in Figure 18. Only among the lower-class whites is there a reversal of the prediction (42 to 51%), and this difference is much smaller than those in the predicted direction. More striking is the new finding that the matriarchal situation differs very little from the "strong-male" pattern in rates of self-disparagement, after race and social class have been taken into account. In fact, four of the six comparisons between columns 4 and 5 of Figure 18 show students in the "strong-male" households as having slightly *higher* rates of self-disparagement than in the matriarchy. This may indicate that the latter is associated with a relatively low degree of *realism* in the children's self-evaluations, perhaps as a result of the mothers' attempts to protect them by sugar-coating harsh realities. Presence of a father figure, whether working or not, may bring about a more critical and realistic balance in interaction and interpretations that contribute to the child's developing self-conceptions. The added factor, the father's unemployment, may tip the balance toward negative images of the boy's prospective self and may confirm the girl's fear that her future marriage partner will probably be an inadequate breadwinner. Naturally, in analyses and arguments involving the effects on children of missing, weak, or otherwise negative male role models in the family, thorough attention may be paid to questions of the acquisition of sex roles (Kagan, 1964). The Coleman Study contained no material on this subject nor were the methods used in it appropriate to the depth analysis that would be necessary. This, in addition to the fact that the sex of the student makes little if any difference in terms of the relations described above, led me to ignore this entire field of research.

To summarize the discussion in relation to hypothesis 13: the data of Coleman's Study do support the proposition that family role structure is associated with favorability of self-conception even when race and social class have been taken into account: the patterns of association are fairly consistent, but very weak. In general, the "strong-male" and matriarchal configurations show frequencies of self-rejection that are low in about equal degree, while the "weak-male" and "neither-parent-present" patterns tend to substantially higher rates. The specific nature of the relation varies somewhat from one aspect of self-conception to another, and in most cases is only roughly linear. Great care will have to be exercised in building this set of relations into a more general model of the ways in which family structure and the other factors shape aspiration.

Hypothesis 14: Family Role Structure and Aspiration

Hypothesis 14 is that family role structure will be related to the various forms of aspiration. More specifically, it is anticipated that family structure will be found positively related to the level of achievement and aspiration tapped in the Coleman data, even after race and social class have been taken into account. This pattern is expected to parallel that observed with self-conception: "weak-male," matriarchy and "strong-male" configurations respectively associated with lower, medium, and higher aspirations. All of this is based on assumptions about the functions of interpersonal security, material resources, and symbolic role modeling and draws upon a wide range of existing literature (Parsons and Bales, 1955; Turner, 1964; Douvan and Adelson, 1966: ch. 2-5; Barnard, 1966; Liebow, 1966; Pavenstedt *et al.,* 1967; Lidz, 1969; and Bandura, 1969).

This hypothesis receives strong support from the cross-tabulation patterns of the family structure variable with each of the measures of aspiration. Before introducing race or class controls, we find the following relationships with family structure: high school program (D = +.40***), occupational expectation (+.21***), overall grade average (+.18***), desire for education (+.17***), college plans (+.12***), and how good a student the respondent wants to be (+.03). In all six cases the "strong-male" configuration reaches the highest levels of aspiration, the matriarchy the intermediate levels, and the "weak-male" situation shows distinctly the lowest, exactly as predicted in hypotheses 14.

Controlling race only reveals that the relationship between family structure and aspiration is usually stronger among whites than among blacks, especially in those measures that concern achievement closer at hand. Examples are:

desire for education (+.21*** among whites and +.13** among blacks), and grade average (+.22*** among whites and .06 among blacks). This is one more indication that, in addition to race, factors of social structure are very difficult for blacks to overcome, even with the support of the more stable family configurations.

When social class is introduced as a control, however, the emerging patterns are far less simple, and they require graphic presentation before the hypothesis can be assessed. Figure 19 portrays the relation of family structure to educational and occupational aspiration, according to social class and race.

Nine of the twelve patterns show a positive relation between family role structure and aspiration. These range from an essentially zero relation (+.002 in lower-class whites on desire for education) to a respectable +.26 in middle-class blacks on occupational expectation. Of the three negative relations, only the —.10 of the lower-class whites on occupational expectation is of even noticeable size, and it is entirely the result of the unusual fact that the students in the "strong-male" category are *less* likely than those in the matriarchy to express a high occupational expectation (11% to 27%).

More generally, the "strong-male" pattern has either a higher proportion of high aspiration than does the matriarchal configuration (in 5 comparisons) or an essentially equal proportion (in 6 comparisons). The positive differences are largest in the middle-class black students, perhaps indicating that the mother alone has difficulty in communicating with her children about the actual possibilities of the world of work.

Empirical support for hypothesis 14 is strongest among the middle-class black students (D = +.20 on educational aspiration, +.26 on occupational expectation). The percentages among them reporting that they expect to enter a professional or managerial occupation are: "neither-parent-present," 0%; "weak-male," 25%; matriarchy, 34%; and "strong-male," 53%. Here it is probable that the economically weak male provides a negative or counter-model, in contrast to the clear occupational attainment of the mother. The "weak-male" configuration does not differ much from the "strong-male" pattern except in the cases of working-class and lower-class whites where students in the "weak-male" family show, respectively, lower proportions and somewhat higher proportions of high aspiration. This may be accounted for by the unemployed white father who projects career fantasies upon his children, as contrasted with the sporadically employed male model who works only at the most menial jobs and presents a stark actuality.

The "neither-parent-present" configuration generally has the lowest proportion of high aspiration (9 out of 10 comparisons). Although cases are very few, this pattern may be seen to produce a resigned and pessimistic view of the future, pointing once again to the importance of role models in the developing of a conception of the future self. While the correlation observed between family structure and aspiration are very small, their substantial consistency leads to the conclusion that hypothesis 14 is supported in direction but with very little potency, except in key groups such as the middle-class blacks.

Hypothesis 15: Measured Verbal Ability and Aspiration

Perhaps it is a reflection of the ideological rejection of "individual traits" in favor of "social characteristics," that a measurement of mental ability is rarely included in sociological research on educational or occupational aspirations. A few recent studies in which some steps have been taken toward

Figure 19—Family structure and aspirations, by social class and race.

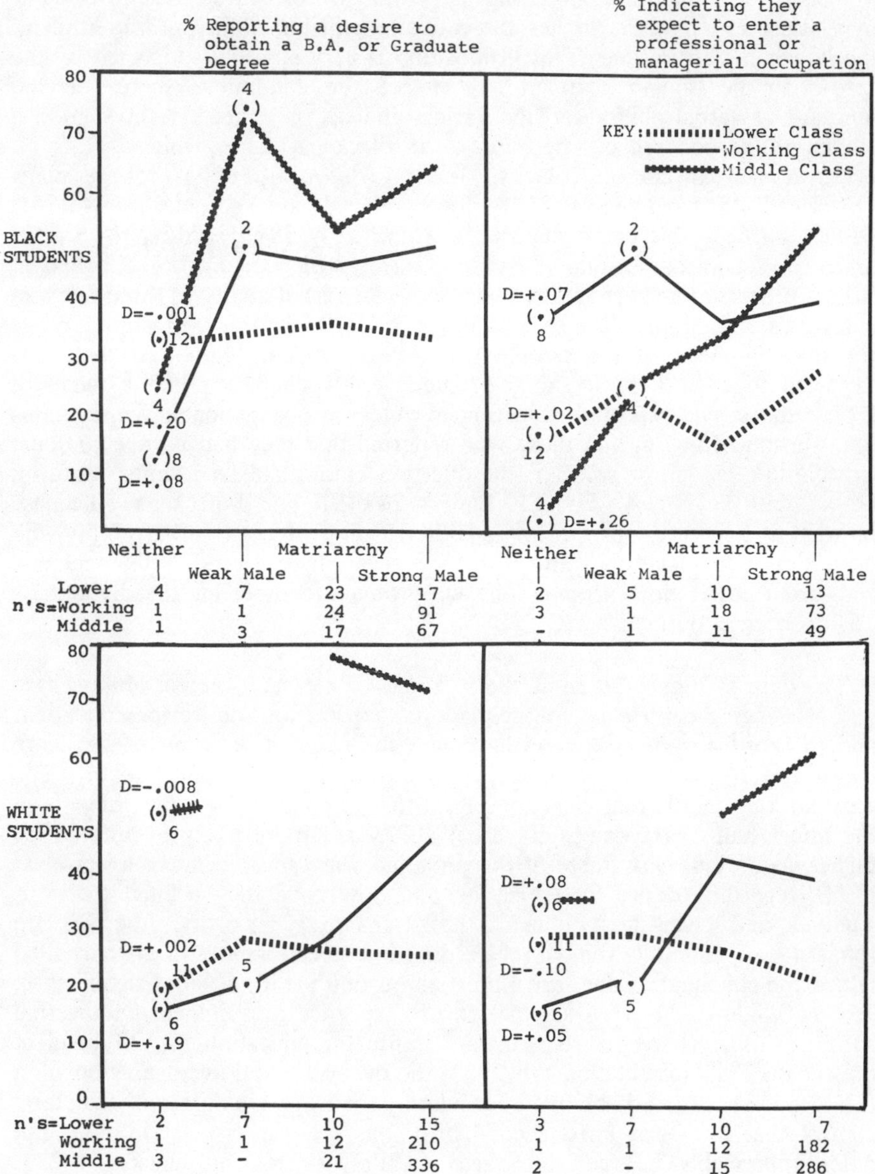

assessing the importance of this ill-defined but clearly relevant dimension (cf. Flanagan, *et al.*, 1962; Eckland, 1965; Sewall and Shah, 1967; Duncan, Haller, and Portes, 1968) emphasize the fact that mental ability, while typically related to socioeconomic status at approximately the +.30 level, does have its own relation also to level of aspiration. The Sewall and Shah study indicates that this second, independent relationship is usually of a slightly greater magnitude than the first (1967:17).

Fortunately, the Coleman Study did include a measure of at least the verbal aspects of developed mental ability, and these scores can be used to test our hypothesis 15: that the higher the measured mental ability of the student, the higher his aspirations. This proposition is very strongly supported by the zero-order Pearsonian correlations between the continuous scores on the measure of verbal ability and the various indices of aspiration: how good a student the respondent says he wants to be (blacks, +.23**, whites, +.35**); occupational expectation (blacks, +.33*, whites, +.36**); college plans (blacks, +.25**, whites, +.44**); over-all grade average (blacks, +.25**, whites, +.42**); educational desire (blacks, +.38**, whites, +.51**); and high school curriculum (blacks, +.42**, whites, +.38**). Looked at from a different perspective, the mean score on verbal ability of three relevant categories of aspiration are seen to differ in just the predicted fashion. While the over-all mean of the sample was 269.3, students who said that they expected to enter a professional or managerial occupation had a mean of 275.6; those who reported expecting to enter an occupation lower in status had a mean of 267.6, and those who reported that they had no occupational expectation, as yet, or who left the question blank, had an average score on verbal ability of 262.4 ($F = 130.1$, $df = 2\&1481$, $p < .0001$). Yet because of what is known about the mutual interrelation of both verbal ability and aspiration with social class and with race, these striking gross differences and zero-order correlations are not sufficient grounds for inferring that hypothesis 15 has been confirmed here.

The data of Figure 20 show the relations of measured verbal ability, race and class being controlled, to occupational expectation, desire for education, and to expression of how good a student the respondent wants to be. Here hypothesis 15 continues to receive very strong and consistent support. The most striking fact is that in *every one* of the 18 comparisons, the students in the upper half of the range of verbal ability are more likely to specify the higher aspiration. Only three of the differences are small (among lower-class blacks regarding desire for education and how good they wanted to be as students, and lower-class whites on the latter issue); all of the other D's are robust ($\geq +.18$) and even with the reduced numbers of cases in the partialled tables, the chi-square values are almost all beyond the .01 level of significance. Second, while the average association of excellence as a student with verbal ability (+.16) is weaker than that of desire for education (+.29) and of the occupational expectation (+.295), the over-all grand average association ($D = +.25$) is remarkably high considering the extensive degree of structural control that has been introduced. Third, the average association does not differ appreciably between the races (whites, +.26 and blacks, +.23).

Finally, across all three aspirations the white students do not show much variation according to social class (+.23, +.28, and +.27). The black students do show fairly consistent trends: association between level of verbal ability and of aspiration is lowest in the lower class, intermediate in the working class, and highest in the middle class (D = +.12, +.22 and +.37 respectively). Since the absolute level of aspiration among these brighter black

Figure 20—Verbal ability and selected aspirations, by race and social class (all n's large enough for reliable percentaging).

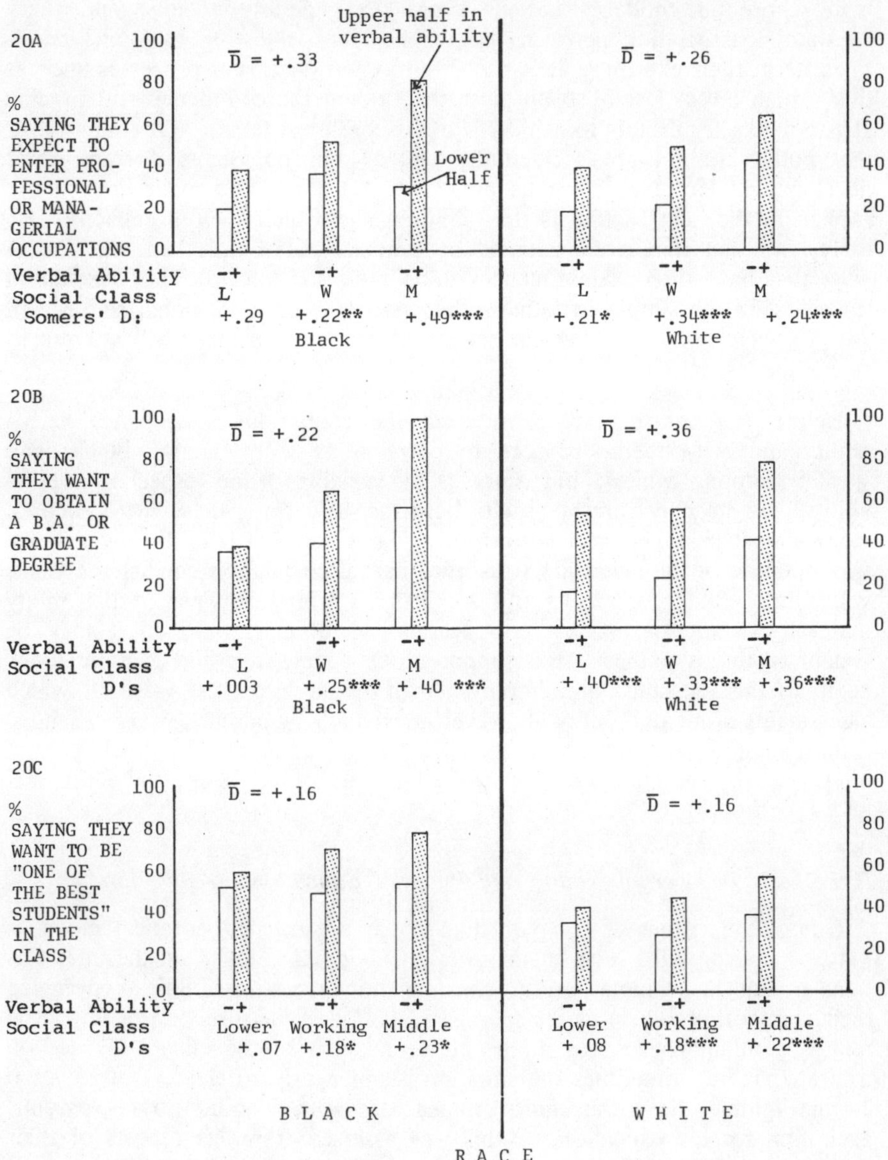

students also is directly correlated with social class (e.g., 36, 50 and 80 percent of whom say that they expect to enter a professional or managerial occupation), it is possible that the black working-class parents and even more so the middle-class parents are especially urging their brighter children toward educational and occupational achievement.

Hypothesis 16: Verbal Ability and Favorability of Self-Conception

Although the impact of mental ability on the nature of the students' developing conceptions of self is not a primary focus, earlier studies of both high school and college students suggest a generally positive and fairly substantial association between these dimensions, allowing for some curvilinearity at their extremes. It is possible to envision casual processes such as that a high level of self-esteem gives the student the confidence and psychic stance necessary if he is to achieve a high score on a test of verbal ability, or that both variables are accidentally-related joint outcomes of some prior development. However, the reasoning hinted at above and made much more explicit in the next section is that children show their mental capacity very early, and that they are evaluated by parents, peers and then teachers in ways that have direct consequences upon their self-esteem. This orientation leads first to the simple hypothesis that verbal ability and global self-esteem are positively related; in the last section of this monograph I will attempt to assess the causal ordering.

Before any controls are introduced, the continuous versions of verbal ability and self-esteem are seen to correlate +.27** among blacks and +.36** among whites, but since both variables (and especially verbal ability) are strongly correlated with both race and class, these two structural factors must be taken into account in judging the worth of the hypothesis. Computation of the necessary first-order partial correlation coefficients yields values of +.24** for blacks and +.32** for whites between verbal ability and self-esteem after taking into account social class, and so it may be concluded that hypothesis 16 is supported. Of course, this finding points once again to the relevance and importance of research on the ways in which assessments of mental ability (however arrived at) by parents, peers, teachers, achievement testers and other agents of socialization are fed back to and interpreted by the child (see especially Deutsch, *et al.,* 1968; and Rosenthal and Jacobson, 1968).

Hypothesis 17: Verbal Ability and Parental Educational Aspiration

One of the virtues of the path diagram as a form of theoretical model is that it encourages the investigator to take explicit account of all the interrelations among the variables, and to consider the various possibilities concerning their temporal sequence or reciprocal effects. Often the direction of impact is relatively unambiguous (as in the above analysis of the effects of race on aspiration), but sometimes the situation is not nearly so clear. Thus relation 16 in Figure 1 links the student's measured verbal ability to his parents' aspiration for his education, as this was assessed from *his* reports of their desires and urgings. However, in addition to the possibility that his report of his parents' behavior may be contaminated with a bias toward his own aspirations, there is the further difficulty of untangling the time order between the manifestation of his ability and his parents' aspirations.

One could argue, as did the Coleman analysts (1966:292-295), that their test is best considered as a measure of verbal *achievement,* and thus of the effectiveness of the child's schooling. This would be to assume that the present level of his verbal capacity, as tested, is a relatively recent outcome of his recent educational experience and other influences in his personal situation, and as these forces change with time, his verbal capacity is likely to vary a good deal, both absolutely and relative to the capacity of others of his age. Inspection of the kinds of items used in the measure of verbal ability and the realization that both the sentence-completion and synonyms sub-test were actually closely-timed power tests lead to a more plausible interpretation of the meaning of the scores: that the scores on verbal skills reflect a *slowly* developing and fairly stable ability to manipulate cognitively a body of moderately abstract cultural signs and meanings, within a strictly limited time and under the rigid and formal conditions characteristic of mass testing. Mental skills of this kind, then, are better regarded as outcomes of the exceedingly complex interaction of the child's biological endowment, his family's emotional and symbolic richness, and a very wide range of physical, psychological, sub-cultural, and social structural factors that begin to exert an effect long before the time of formal schooling. Later, these developed cognitive capacities or "meta-skills" determine substantially the manner in which the child deals with classroom interaction and educational content. To the degree that stratification and ethnic sub-cultural factors affect the development of mental ability long before he enters school, one would expect that the macrostructural categories would account for as much or even more of the variance in scores on measured verbal ability than do the various features of the school environment included in the Coleman study. This is exactly what was found (Coleman, 1966:299, Table 3.221.1, ninth-grade section): all of the many school-related factors *in total* accounted for only 8.96% of the variance in verbal ability in the case of northern black students and 8.31% in the case of northern whites, as compared to the 21.52% among blacks and 31.25% among whites attributable to the combination of objective background factors, parental interest and desire for offspring's education, and "child's attitudes" (interest in school, academic self-conception, and sense of control over the environment). These and related findings led the Coleman analysts to this frank but embarrassing conclusion:

> School to school variations in achievement, from whatever source (community differences, variations in the average home background of the student body, or variations in school factors), are much smaller than individual variations within the school, at all grade levels, for all racial and ethnic groups. This means that most of the variation in achievement could not possibly be accounted for by school differences, since most of it lies within the school.

* * *

Thus the larger part of school-to-school variation in achievement appears to be not a consequence of effects of school variations at all, but of variations in family backgrounds of the entering student bodies.

A reasonable conclusion is, then, that our schools have great uniformity insofar as their effect on the learning of pupils is concerned. The data suggest that variations in school quality are not highly related to variations in achievement of pupils (*ibid.,* pp. 296-297).

On the contrary, however, if provisionally we entertain the assumption that current tests of verbal ability measure a capacity that began to develop at the child's conception and has been undergoing a slow and stable process of growth under the encouraging or discouraging influence of family, peer, neighborhood, social class, race and other sub-cultural factors, we can treat the *present* scores, relative to the *present* grade cohort, as rough estimations of each child's *earlier* standing, relative to his *previous* cohort. Of course, it is recognized that estimations of earlier relative standing on verbal ability are imperfect and not inadequate substitutes for measures taken before the child entered school. Yet the general dimension of mental ability is of such great importance in reaching anything like a comprehensive model of the aspiration and role acquisition process, and the possibility of error is so greatly reduced by the use of dichotomized present scores to estimate into which half of the range of mental ability the student would have fallen if relevant tests had been administered in the preschool years, that I decided to proceed with the analysis on this imperfect but potentially fruitful basis.

Hypothesis 17 is that the higher the measured verbal ability of the student, the higher his parents' aspiration for his education. It could be argued that having parents who stress the value and importance of educational attainment should motivate students to perform well on tests of this sort, and in fact this argument is fundamental to our interpretation of verbal ability. However, it should be remembered that the urgings and desires of parents reported by the students that result in high scores on the index of parental aspiration concern elements of educational attainment that are likely to be rather late in appearing, much later than the mental facility that the present measure is being used to estimate. These elements are reports by the student that his father and his mother have expressed to him their desire that he be "one of the best students in the class" and that he should achieve a B.A. or graduate degree. Since these students are now in the ninth-grade and since most are fourteen-year-olds, it seems fairly reasonable to assume that these rather specific desires have been communicated to them at a point in time *later* than that at which the parents began to form opinions about their developing mental ability. The assumption is that parents are more likely to focus their aspirations for their offsprings' achievement and mobility, both fantasy and more realistic aims on their abler children than on children who show signs of difficulty and probable failure. This is not to say that parents do not frequently indulge the human propensity to idealize both the future and their children by spinning romantic fabrications, even for the least able—only that the tendency is to communicate high educational aspirations more frequently to the more able children.

That the empirical data provide fairly strong support for this contention is shown in the substantial correlation between the continuous version of the scale of verbal ability and the full index of parental aspirations (blacks, r = +.29**, and whites, +.40**). Yet because social class is related to both verbal ability (blacks, +.25**, whites, +.43**), and parental aspiration (blacks, +.23**, whites, +.30**), a controlled cross-tabulation sequence should reveal whether the hypothesized relation between ability and parental aspiration might be spurious. The partial correlations of verbal ability and parental aspiration after taking account of social class are still quite substantial (blacks, +.24, whites, +.31). The fact that the relation is higher in the case of whites (as was so also of the correlation between verbal ability and self-esteem) probably means that this kind of school-oriented ability is more consistently stressed and rewarded in white families, while the black students are subjected to more conflicting and negative influences.

Figure 21 shows the mean value of the index of parental aspiration among students in the lower half of the scores on verbal ability as contrasted with the mean among those in the higher half, with separate plots for the three social classes. This procedure gives rather conservative results because for purposes of the cross-tabulations from which these figures and the values of Somers' D were calculated the index of parental aspirations was trichotomized (a value of 1 being assigned to the lower third, 2 to the middle third, and 3 to the upper third), and because contrasting the entire low and high halves of the range of ability yields much less striking differences than would comparing just the upper and lower thirds. The procedure does, however, have the advantage of using all the cases.

Inspection of the plotted values of the parental aspiration 3-point index and comparison of the value of Somers' D in each social class reveal that the originally obtained relationship between ability and parental aspiration (D = +.27*** in the uncontrolled table) holds up undiminished among the middle-class students (blacks, D = +.29*** and whites, +.34***) and and is still appreciable in the working-class sample (blacks, +.19*, whites, +.24***) but declines in the lower class (blacks, —.06, whites, +.14).

One possible interpretation of the lack of the predicted relation in the lower class might be that so many of these students score in the lower half of the range of verbal ability (90% of the black students, 77% of the white students) and so few of the parents, when categorized in terms of educational aspiration, fall into the upper third of the total distribution (24% of black students and 15% of white), that those who are reported in the habit of urging education on their children may be engaged to a degree greater than usual in fantasy.

Since in the bulk of the sample the pattern of results does fall in the predicted direction and the over-all measures of association yield reasonable values, even after taking account of race and social class (weighted average D = +.23), it can be concluded that hypothesis 16 has consistent support as regards all but the lower-class students. Now that verbal ability has been shown to be related to parents' aspiration, it remains to show the degree to which the latter is connected to the students' aspirations toward achievement.

Figure 21—Verbal ability and level of parental education aspiration, according to social class and race.

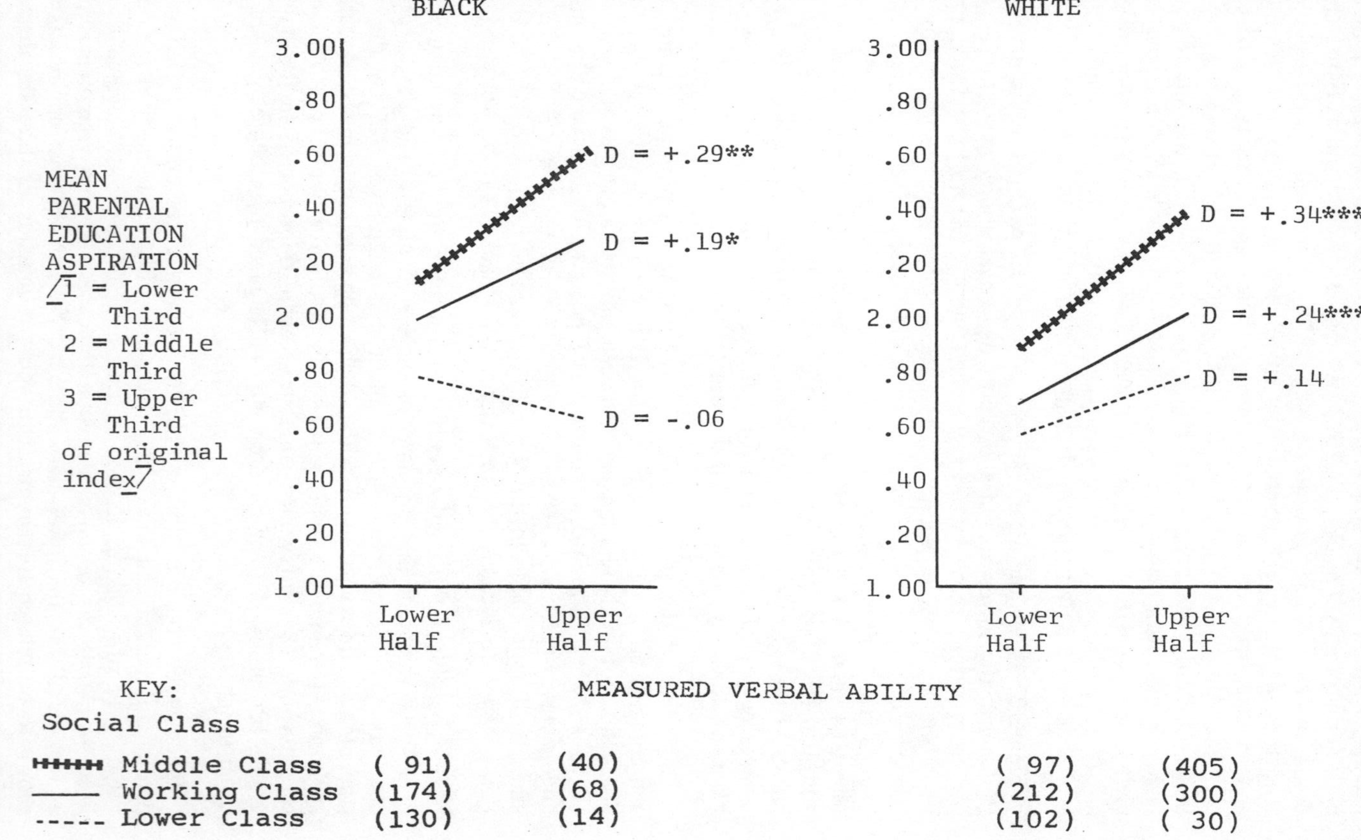

Hypothesis 18: Parental aspiration and students' aspiration

Hypothesis 18 is that the higher the level of parental educational aspiration, the higher the students' own aspiration. It is based on a wide range of previous research, especially the work of Kahl (1953), Rosen (1956, 1959, 1961), Bordua (1960), Elder (1962b), and Sewell and Shah (1968), as well as on the general conclusions of the diverse studies reviewed by Goldstein (1967:20-81, 136-210) and collected in Rosen, Crockett and Nunn (1969). In addition to the theoretical grounds for the hypothesis supplied by the literature—social learning, role modeling, anticipatory socialization and the like—there are other reasons to expect that there will be a substantial correlation between what a ninth-grader says are his own aspirations and what he attributes to his parents. The general phenomenon of reducing cognitive incongruity is involved, whether we are dealing with a student who overstates his own aspirations to match the high standards he sees his parents cherish for him; or with one who understates his parents' desires to make them correspond to his own ambitions and thereby feels less of a traitor to his family; or, finally, with the one who is ashamed to admit such traitorous fantasies and so reports that his own desires match the more modest plans of his parents more closely than they actually do.

Although the items making up the various indices of student aspiration and parental urging were fairly well scattered throughout the questionnaire, the psychic overlap in content was obvious, and it seemed appropriate to forego statements of one-way causal determination in favor of the less demanding interpretation of mutual interrelation. Thus the following presentation will make use of the measure Tau C, which is one useful cross-tabulation analog of the Pearsonian r in that it makes no assumptions of causal direction. As does r, Tau C can range from +1.00 to —1.00. It assumes an order in the categories of the row and column variables, and is generally roughly equal in magnitude to r. Tau C has the advantage over other table measures of association in that it does not require that the number of rows and columns in the table be equal. As was the convention when reporting the degree of association by use of Somers' D, I have appended one, two, or three stars to the reported Tau C value to indicate the chi-square level of *in*significance of the table on which the measure was computed (*=p <.05; **=p<.01; *** = p<.001).

Before applying the race and class controls called for in the hypothesis, we find that parental educational aspiration is positively and very strongly related to how good a student the respondent says he wants to be (Tau C = +.54***), also to whether he has taken active steps to enroll in a college-preparatory curriculum (+.26***), to the grade average he reports having received in the previous year (+.30***), to his own desire for education (+.63***), to his declared plans to go to college (+.49***), and, finally, to his level of occupational expectation (+.20***).

Figure 22 shows that the hypothesized relation of parental educational aspiration to the three most important aspirations of the student holds up even after application of the race and social-class controls. These controls made the least difference regarding students' avowed desire to be one of the best in the class (Figure 22A). Among middle-class whites, where the relation is strongest (Tau C = +.59***), a student whose parents score high on this index is over seven times as likely to report this aspiration as is one whose parents score low. Even where the relation is weakest (lower-class blacks, Tau C = +.41***), those whose parents are high scorers are over twice as likely to report that they themselves want to be one of the best in the class.

When attention is turned to the percentage of students who express a desire to graduate from a four-year college or obtain a graduate degree (Figure 22B), race and social class are seen to make almost no difference in cases where parental aspiration is low (these students fall into the range

Figure 22—Relation of parental educational aspiration index to selected student aspirations, by race and social class.

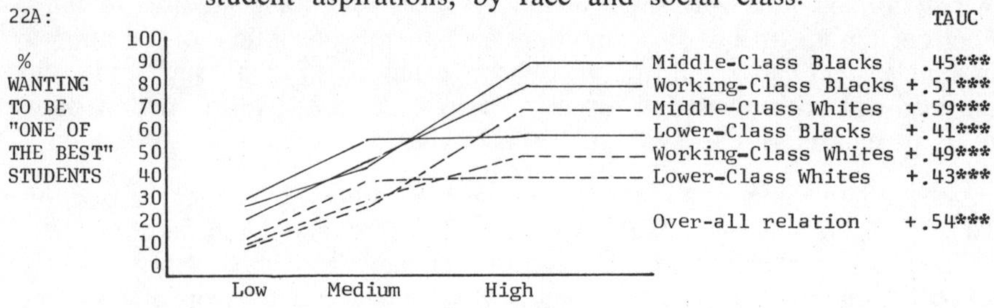

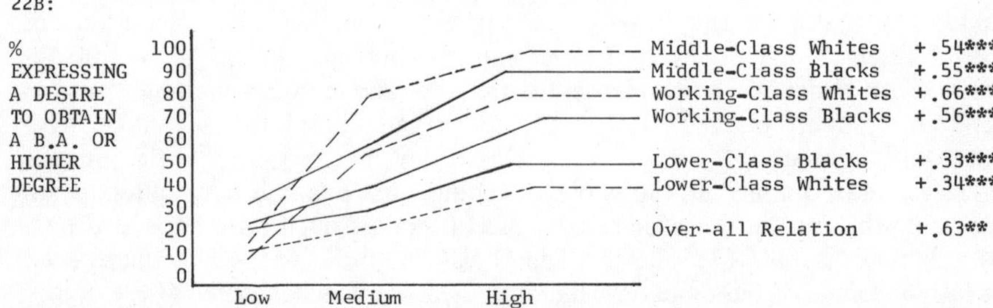

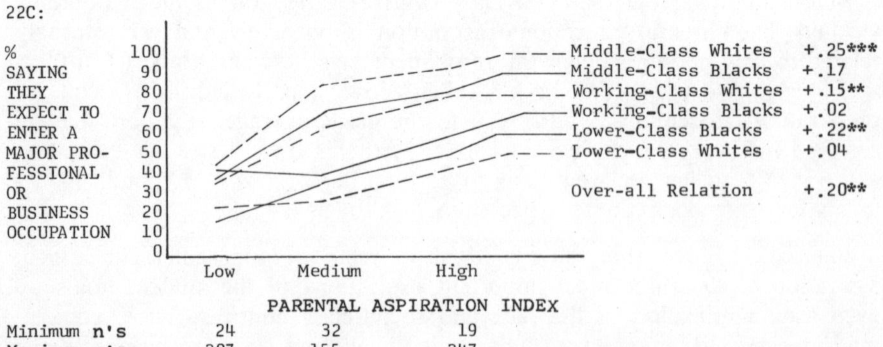

	Low	Medium	High
Minimum n's	24	32	19
Maximum n's	207	155	247

from 10 to 25%), but they do introduce appreciable variation in cases where parental aspiration is medium or high (from 35 to 75% and from 60 to 94%, respectively). Where the relation is weakest (lower-class blacks, Tau C = +.33***), those with high-aspiring parents are still over 2.7 times as likely to desire higher education as are those whose parents score low.

The relationship to occupational expectation (Figure 22C) was weakest initially (Tau C = +.20***), and most affected by introduction of the controls. Variation in percentage of students indicating that they expect to enter a professional or managerial occupation is large where parental aspiration is high (ranging from 25 to 73%). In two of the control categories, lower-class whites (+.04) and working-class blacks (+.02), the original relationship disappears completely; both groups show some slight curvilinearity in the relation such that students with "medium" parents aspire to advanced education a little less frequently than do those whose parents score either low or high on the index.

Since in 16 of the 18 instances the predicted relationship holds up even after the introduction of race and class controls, a basis has been provided for inferring that a positive and rather substantial relation does exist between the educational aspirations of the parents and the students' own aspirations, especially to advanced education.

Hypothesis 19: Parental aspiration and self-conception

Much the same line of reasoning that supported the hypothesis of a positive relationship between aspirations of parents and those of the student provides the ground for hypothesizing that parental aspirations also are strongly related to favorability of the student's self-conception. Furthermore, we are again faced with the difficulty that the predominant causal sequencing in the development of these two dimensions is not clear. In many instances it is likely that early development in the child of a favorable conception of self (especially regarding self-determination or academic competence) stimulates visions of high academic attainment in his parents. But for two reasons suggest that the reverse is more likely. First, many parents entertain the thought of a college education for their child even before he is born, communicating this to him (as argued above) as he begins to show convincing signs of mental aptitude even in the preschool period. Second, an expanding body of theory and research on the development of self-conception indicates that the more generalized and inferential aspects of self such as the sense of competence or of self-determination become increasingly clearer after the period of latency, as the child moves away from the confines of the family and into the instrumental and competitive world of junior high school and high school (cf. Gordon and Gergen, 1968: Part IV; Rosenberg 1963; Gordon, 1969).

If this line of reasoning is valid, it can be concluded provisionally that the parents' dreams for the child's future, based partly on their idea of, first, his mental ability and, second, on their perception of the relevant opportunity structures, play an important role in shaping their feelings about him and their encouragement in him of self-mastery and independence. Their aspirations thus ultimately have an effect upon the child's own feelings about himself. Naturally, this is a complex interaction in which the parents' aspirations, the child's ability, his self-conceptions, and, finally, his aspirations are all interwoven. Thus, if the parents' aspirations are high but the child's mental ability is low, he will very probably feel ashamed of any shortcomings in school work and will lose some measure of his sense of competence and of self-esteem, whether or not he lowers his aspirations. To complicate matters even further, the fact that he recognizes that he is not going to live up to the aspirations of his parents may reduce his sense of competence and self-esteem (if he has deeply internalized his parents' expectations) but may simultaneously strengthen his feeling of autonomy or freedom from control by others. Only much more subtle longitudinal research can even hope to unravel these skeins of reciprocal and interacting relationships.*

Since it is assumed that the parents' aspirations take form and are expressed before the students begin to develop their own relatively abstract self-conceptions partially on the basis of the parental aspirations and expectations (in combination with their symbolic interpretation of how their ability is rewarded in terms of grades, peer acceptance, family support, etc.), the one-way or asymmetric measure of ordered-category association (Somers' D) is used in the analysis.

Before race and social class are controlled, the index of parental aspirations shows small to moderate association with the dimensions of self-conception: D = +.11*** with basic self-acceptance, +.29*** with self-rated brightness, +.17*** with academic competence, +.22*** with general competence, +.19*** with self-determination, and +.25*** with global self-esteem. Before it can be concluded that the positive relation stated in hypothesis 19 between parental aspiration and the various dimensions of self-conception does in fact exist, it is necessary to control the possibility that social class and measured verbal ability (which have been shown to be related positively and substantially to both parental aspiration and favorability of self-conception) may be producing the apparent pattern of relationship. The data in Figure 23 are arranged to facilitate inference about the relationship between parental aspiration and global self-esteem, after the relation of each to social class and verbal ability has been taken into account. Race is not used in these comparisons because it is not appreciably related to parental aspiration nor to global self-esteem. Once again, the somewhat more valid proportion of respondents scoring *low* on the index of global self-esteem is the dependent variable, and the denotations, "brighter" and "less bright," refer to the student's position above or below the common median (269).

---

* A longitudinal study, although not a particularly subtle one, is the present author's attempt to trace changes accompanying retirement in terms of the identical dimensions of self-conception: the systemic senses of competence, self-determination, unity, moral worth, personal autonomy, and the more global evaluative dimension, self-esteem. This is a three-phase panel study, supported by the National Institute of Mental Health, and involving detailed interviews and a questionnaire on self-conception administered to some 300 persons 6 months before the date of retirement, at one month after and again eight months after retirement. (Gordon, 1968a, 1968c).

Inspection of Figure 23 reveals that the original relation between parental aspiration and global self-esteem (D = +.25***) holds up in four of the six sub-group plots. Even in the two cases where the linear association is reduced (lower class, less bright, +.08; middle class, less bright, +.10), the pattern is still in the predicted direction. Moreover, the relation is strongest among the brighter students, ranging from +.18** in the middle class, to +.25*** in the working class and to a high of +.38* among the few lower-class students who scored above the median on verbal ability. This last finding suggests that brighter students, relatively disadvantaged as to family status and material resources, are more dependent upon their parents' emotional and symbolic support than are those more favorably situated. Also, the finding that the working class less bright students are still susceptible to this kind of parental influence (+.19*) suggests a condition which might be described as a watershed between the lower class, where the parents' encouragement of education reached a high level in only 19% of the less bright, and the middle class, where 34% report an equal amount of urging.

Figure 23—Parental aspiration and global self-esteem, by social class and measured verbal ability.

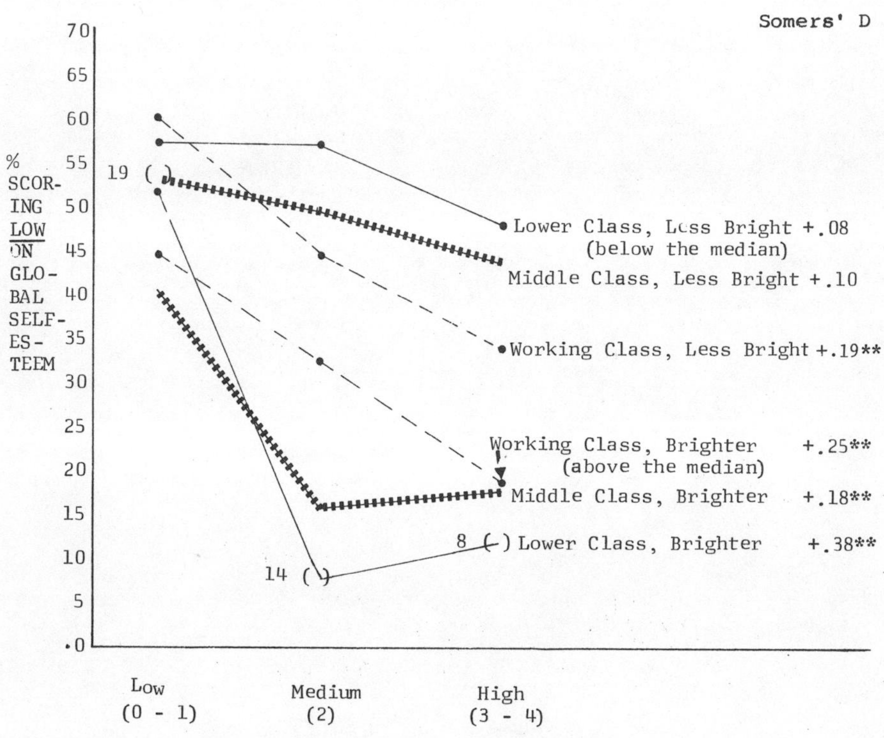

( ) indicates that base n for percentage is less than 30; exact figure given at side.

On the basis of these comparisons and observed associations, I infer that the level of reported parental educational aspiration is positively related to self-conception, even after social class and measured verbal ability have been appropriately controlled.

V

V. SELF-CONCEPTION AND ASPIRATION

There has been relatively little theoretical formulation and almost no empirical evidence concerning the crucial question of the impact of self-conceptions on the motivation and direction of subsequent conduct (noted in *The Self in Social Interaction,* Gordon and Gergen, eds., 1968, cf., introduction to Part V, "Self-conception and the determination of behavior," pp. 281-390). The great preponderance of previous work has focused on either the nature of particular aspects of self-conception, or on how these may be related to selected features of the individual's socialization or current situation (Wylie, 1961). Some of the major exceptions to this trend (Gordon and Gergen, *ibid.,* Part IV) are summarized briefly here because on them is based the major hypothesis of this study: the more favorable the student's self-conceptions, the higher his aspiration.

Thorstein Veblen was one of the earliest social analysts to point out the unending desire to maintain and enhance one's level of self-esteem as being one of several motives underlying development of exploitative prowess and acquisition of property for the sake of its symbolic importance (*The Theory of the Leisure Class,* 1899). Maintenance of the self was put forward as a major human motive in the slender but important writings of Prescott Lecky, who in his *Self-Consistency: A Theory of Personality* (1945; esp. 19, 42-50, 82-89, and appendix III) argues that much of human conduct (motivated acts rather than forced movements) is "in character" because of the individual's attempts to render his world *meaningful, consistent,* and *predictable* by acting and making choices so as to maintain the structure of values he has developed. The most important of the values define his roles in life and the kind of person he is, furnishing him with appropriate standards of conduct. The premises that idealized role-identities form major aspects of self-structure and provide action with both general motivation and specific guidance have been incorporated into the most recent explorations of the relations between self and role (McCall and Simmons, 1966; Turner, 1966; Gordon, 1969).

Theories of the consistency of attitude and behavior have occasionally been invoked to provide the link between maintenance of self-esteem (or some other aspect of self-conception) and such diverse outcomes as changing behavior so as to elicit more favorable or at least more congruent responses from significant others (Backman, Secord, and Peirce, 1963), changing behavior and self-evaluation so as to increase the validity of the conception of the self (Pepitone, 1968), being influenced or persuaded by others in social interaction (Cohen, 1959), and many forms of psychological selectivity (Rosenberg, 1967). Concerning emotive relations with others, Fromm (1939) asserted self-love to be the basis of love for others rather than the reverse, and Rogers (1950) marshalled evidence to support the argument that when therapy increases positive self-regard the result is lowered psychological tension and a decrease in many kinds of defensive behavior.

On a more social level, Goffman (1955, 1959) has outlined some of the ways in which a person's presented images of self operate as crucial elements to himself and to others in the ensuing interaction. Shibutani (1961: especially 87-95), following George Herbert Mead, has formulated these current self-conceptions and the self-images imaginatively attributed to relevant others as the self-control basis of social control.

Yet much less theoretical or empirical work has been done regarding possible links between current self-conceptions and aspiration. Quite an extreme position on the relationship between self-conception and conduct is that taken by Combs and Snygg (1948):

> What a person thinks and how he behaves are largely determined by the concepts he holds about himself and his abilities. . . . How we act in any given situation will be dependent upon (1) how we perceive ourselves, and (2) how we perceive the situation in which we are involved. (p. 122)

And specifically on goals:

> In later life these expectancies form the individual's level of aspiration. Depending upon the concept of self possessed by the individual, he will choose this goal or that as appropriate for such a person as he regards himself to be. . . . Whatever goals are considered worthy of the individual's consideration are dependent upon the way in which he regards himself and the kinds of self expectancies he has acquired in the course of his experience. (p. 140)

Morris Rosenberg reports from his study of some 5,000 New York State high school juniors and seniors (1965:224-230) that those low in self-esteem want to avoid occupations involving subordination or superordination or competition. In addition, he found that those scoring low in self-esteem are about as likely as those scoring high to want to succeed in life, but much less likely to feel that they will in fact do so (pp. 230-232). Also relating aspects of self-conception to occupational aspiration are Backman and Secord (1968), who found that preference for particular occupations among a small sample of college students is related to congruence between their own conceptions of self and what they feel are typical profiles of encumbents of the given occupations, describing them as "confident," "sociable," "unselfish," etc.

The literature on laboratory studies of aspiration-setting yields the prediction that self-esteem is positively related to the level of aspired accomplishment (Lewin, *et al.,* 1944). It should be noted, however, that most of the formulations assess self-esteem in terms of personal *abilities,* and the goals in terms of *difficulty,* to be overcome by skill and/or effort.

A much more subtle interpretation is that drawn from the symbolic interactionist tradition, especially from William James, and perhaps most comprehensively stated by Shibutani in his chapter "Self-esteem and social control" (1961:432-467). Shibutani interprets self-esteem as a much more global and evaluative sense of personal worth, tied to specific abilities only indirectly, if at all. More relevant, too, are the symbolic definitions of significant others as these are related to worth, success, prestige, and the culturally standardized "appropriate" directions and levels of aspiration, regardless of difficulty. But since the possible roles themselves are rated in terms of prestige and other verbally communicated qualities, there may be a tendency toward cognitive balance between the sense of personal worth (as shaped by past evaluations) and the level of the roles aspired to.

As Shibutani is careful to note, however, a substantial body of evidence from psychological sources indicates that in some cases high goals and exceptionally strong "ego-strivings" may also be mechanisms whose function is to compensate for very *low* levels of self-esteem. In his work during the early 1930's (1956: esp. ch. 4), Alfred Adler put this in terms of inferiority feelings and compensatory strivings for superiority. Karen Horney (1945) described the "idealized self-image" as one source of unrealistic goal orientation, and Arthur Cohen (1959) used this formulation in his experiments in communication. These explanations in terms of compensation may perhaps be most helpful in explaining unusually high levels of aspiration, mobility into elites, and the compulsive drive to achieve, symbolized at Harvard in the slurring remark, "He's a complete grind."

This and other lines of reasoning (Shibutani, 1961:432-434) led to the expectation of several departures from a strictly linear relationship between self-esteem and aspiration, and, indeed, Rosenberg has suggested much the same thing regarding the relation between self-esteem and concern with political affairs (1965:ch. 11). While those lowest in self-esteem are likely to feel that they are completely worthless and in a hopeless situation, others, somewhat less despairing, may perceive achievement, superiority, and social mobility as possible routes to self-enhancement; thus they may aspire *higher* and put forth more effort than those who stand moderately high in self-esteem. If those who score highest on a scale of self-esteem because of social desirability or some compensatory factor are screened from the others, they will presumably be found to rank highest also in aspiration—a supposition confirmed in the findings of Cohen (1959) and Rosenberg (1965:ch. 12): that those high in self-esteem enjoy greater self-confidence, strive harder to achieve, are less sensitive to criticism and failure, and less reluctant to face competition, conflict, and the demands of leadership. It also dovetails nicely with a statement on social mobility by Lipset and Zetterberg (1956:163) incorporating Veblen's hypothesis of a connection between self-esteem and the evaluation of rank or consumption:

> Hence, if the society evaluates a high consumption standard favorably the individual will try to maximize his consumption level, since he thereby maximizes his self-evaluation. This theory can easily be generalized to any other dimension of class. Since any ranking is an evaluation, he tries to maximize his rank. This would go for all the rankings we discussed earlier, that is, occupational, consumption, social, and perhaps also power classes. The basic idea is that persons like to protect their class positions in order to protect their egos, and improve their class positions in order to enhance their egos.

Hypothesis 20: The more favorable the self-conception, the higher the aspiration

The major hypothesis of this investigation, that there is a positive association between self-conception and aspiration, is given consistent and rather strong support by the matrix of zero-order Pearsonian correlations arrayed separately by race in Figure 24.

Several inferences may be drawn from the matrix in Figure 24. First, as stated in hypothesis 20, all 72 of the correlations are positive, ranging from +.07 to +.51**, and all but 6 are significant beyond the .01 level. Second, white students show a consistently higher pattern of correlation (reported grand average, +.20** among blacks, +.26** among whites). Third, self-representation in terms of basic self-acceptance, column 1 (r = .14** in both races), is less strongly related to the various aspirations than are the others. This indicates that at least by the time the child has reached the ninth grade, his conceptions of self have been differentiated in terms of a wider repertoire of competencies from his basic self-acceptance (which presumably developed earlier), and that these wider competencies are more relevant to his major life aspirations. Fourth, as was stated in the original hypothesis, sensed academic competence among the white students is more closely associated with "academic" aspirations (rows A-E, averaging +.27) than with occupational expectation (+.17). On the other hand, among black students the pattern is reversed (+.13 with the academic aspirations and +.21 with occupational expectation). Fifth, the fact that the basic measure of self-acceptance has such small associations with aspirations (ranging from +.12 to +.20 among blacks and +.12 to +.17 among whites, with an average of +.14 for both) leads to the conclusion that this dimension of self-conception probably taps

Figure 24—Intercorrelations of self-conceptions and the measures of aspiration, by race.

(Evaluated by Pearsonian r with one star indicating significance beyond the .05 level and two stars indicating significance beyond the .01 level)

SELF-CONCEPTION DIMENSIONS

ASPIRATIONS		(1) Basic self-acceptance	(2) How bright I am	(3) (4) Academic Competence	(5) Overall Competence	(6) Self-Determination	Global Self-esteem	Average Correlation
(A) How good a student the respondent wants to be	Black	.12*	.15**	.16**	.22**	.22**	.27**	.19**
	White	.12**	.32**	.27**	.32**	.32**	.38**	.29**
(B) High School Program	Black	.12**	.19**	.13**	.17**	.22**	.24**	.18**
	White	.12**	.29**	.19**	.14**	.16**	.23**	.19**
(C) Overall grades last year	Black	.13**	.51**	.10*	.25**	.16**	.23**	.23**
	White	.12**	.48**	.29**	.29**	.23**	.32**	.29**
(D) Student's own desire for education	Black	.20**	.23**	.17**	.12	.18**	.27**	.20**
	White	.16**	.39**	.30**	.29**	.27**	.36**	.30**
(E) College plans	Black	.12*	.10*	.07	.19**	.19**	.20**	.14**
	White	.15**	.33**	.30**	.24**	.24**	.34**	.27**
(F) Occupational expectations	Black	.17**	.38**	.21**	.16**	.21**	.29**	.24**
	White	.17**	.35**	.17**	.25**	.21**	.28**	.24**
Average correlations	B	.14**	.26**	.14**	.18**	.20**	.25**	Grand Averages B .20**
	W	.14**	.36**	.25**	.26**	.24**	.32**	Grand Averages W .26**

ascribed and other qualities that do not stand in close relation to achievement or performance. This interpretation is supported by the fact that basic self-acceptance is most strongly related to those aspirations that are most distant and cloaked in fantasy.

Finally, the various aspirations differ appreciably in their association with favorability of self-conception. The order of their relation to the measure of global self-esteem among white and black students is as follows:

r	*White*	*r*	*Black*
.38	How good a student the respondent wants to be	.29	Occupational expectation
.36	Student's desire for education	.27	How good a student the respondent wants to be
.34	Definiteness of college plans	.27	Student's desire for education
.32	Last year's reported overall grades	.24	High School Program
.28	Occupational expectation	.23	Last year's reported overall grades
.23	High School Program	.20	Definiteness of college plans

The previously observed pattern emerges again: the white students show a stronger association between self-esteem and the set of aspirations and achievement orientations. This probably indicates that in blacks the social-psychological dimensions are overwhelmed by the structural and perceptual barriers to attainment

There is a marked difference in rank-order position of occupational expectation between the two races. Although essentially identical in magnitude of relation to self-esteem (.29 among blacks; in whites, .28), occupational expectation is at the very top of the order among the blacks but second to last among the whites. Actual high school program or track also ranks higher among blacks than among whites, while definiteness of college plans ranks much lower in order among blacks. These findings suggest that orientation to directly occupational achievement is relatively more closely connected to self-evaluation among blacks than among whites; the latter seem to perceive the future rather more in terms of education.

But, as was specified in the hypothesis, the degree of association between self-conception and aspiration must be found to remain substantial even after the introduction of additional measures to control the effects of social class, family structure, verbal ability, and parental aspiration.

In the interest of clarity, class and race are first selected as controls. Two main aspirations have been selected for the controlled analysis: desire for education and occupational expectation. Desire for education as presented in Figure 25A and occupational expectation, presented in Figure 25B, reveal remarkable consistency. In all 12 of the controlled-comparison curves, a positive relationship persists between global self-esteem and aspiration, and in 9 of the 12 the relation is clearly linear. These asymmetrical linear relations regarding occupational expectation range from D = +.14*** among middle-class whites to +.35*** among middle-class blacks.

Even in the three cases where there is some curvilinearity, the number of cases in the "high self-esteem" category is so small, comparatively, that the overall curve still has a weak but positive slope: in relation to education, among working-class blacks (+.17***), and among lower-class blacks (+.10*); in relation to occupational expectation, among lower-class blacks (+.07). These reversals among the particularly disadvantaged black students might be interpreted as reflecting either more realistic aspirations than are found among the blacks who rate lower in self-esteem, or as an unreal and invalid level of self-esteem among those who score high. While the latter interpretation might fit better with the proposition that lower- or working-class black students who score high in self-evaluation are among the most likely

Figure 25—Relation of global self-esteem to aspirations, by race and class.

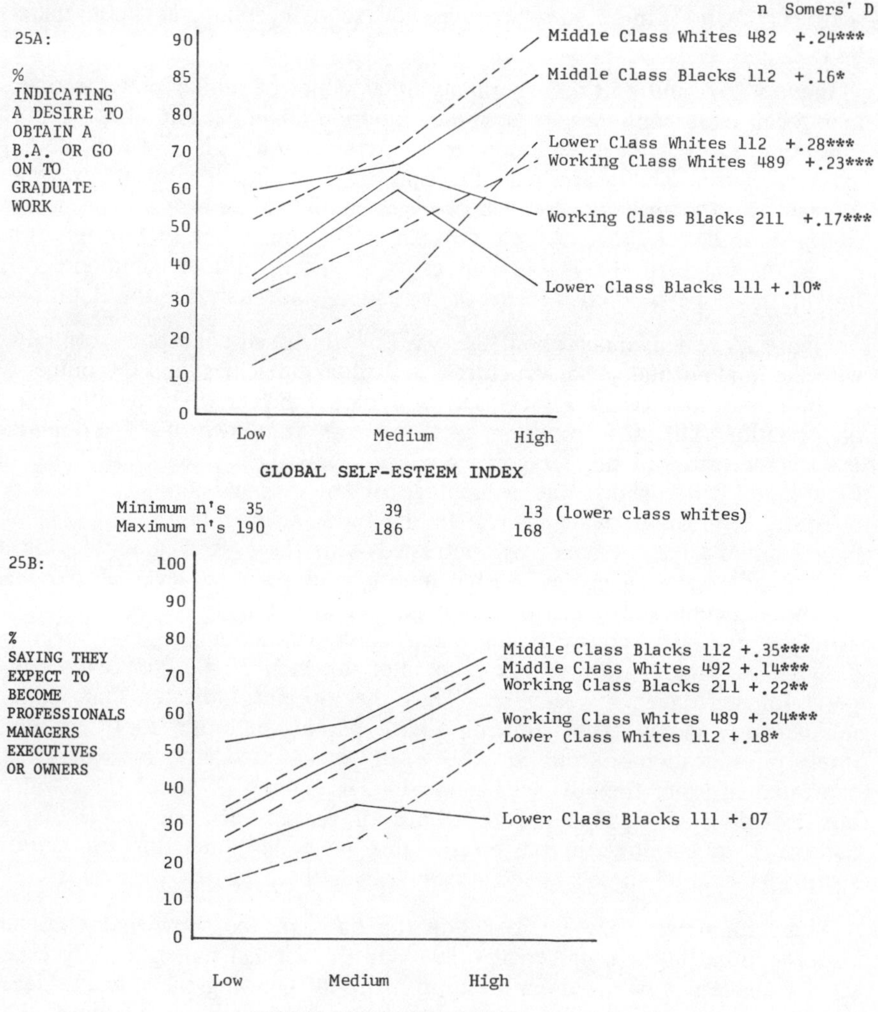

to be compensating for latent feelings of inferiority, only more penetrating research strategies can give the answer.

The relevant sets of tables of the other self-conceptions also show a very consistent tendency for the original uncontrolled or zero-order associations with aspiration to hold up even after partialling by race and social class. Academic competence is least robust in its relation to desire for education, dropping from D = +.21*** to a range of from +.09 to +.21 (averaging about +.16) in the partialled tables. In general, it is among the lower-class students of both races that relationships are found to be weaker than in the whole sample, while the middle-class blacks generally show the strongest relations. Thus, the percentages of the low, medium, and high groupings on self-determination who say that they expect to enter a high prestige occupation are 23, 26, and 39 of lower-class blacks (D = +.06), as against 23, 63, and 74 percent of middle-class blacks (+.40***). This suggests a strong sense of reality; these measurements of self-conception are not merely tapping fantasies.

Figures 25A and 25B and the many other tables of similar patterns reveal that social class continues to be more important than race in shaping both aspiration itself and its relation to self-conception. Thus, when adding measured verbal ability and parental aspirations as further controls, in order to maintain a reasonable number of cases in the tables we will no longer separate the data by race. As will be seen in our concluding section, multiple regression and path analysis models using all these variables simultaneously provide more parsimonious forms of presenting and analyzing the data.

Figure 26 reveals much about the ways in which self-conception combines with the fundamental social structures, individual capacities, and the influence of the family in producing increased explanatory power in predicting levels of aspiration. The most important of the factors from each of these domains (as demonstrated in the foregoing analysis) have been selected for use in Figure 26, which shows the percentage of students indicating a desire to obtain a B.A. or graduate degree among those scoring in the upper third on the index of self-esteem, as contrasted with those scoring in the lower third (social class, measured verbal ability, and reported level of parental aspiration being controlled in each case). The segments of the figure are arranged and grouped by rising social class, verbal ability, and level of parental aspiration, with a three-point plot for each of the contrasted categories of self-esteem in each set. Thus the top line indicates that among middle-class, more verbal students whose parents entertain for them high levels of educational aspiration, 89% of those rated low in self-esteem expressed a desire for advanced education, as against 99% of those rated high, yielding an Epsilon (or difference of proportions) of +.10 and a Somers' D of +.06** in the entire table (n = 244, including the group scoring "medium" in self-esteem) from which these figures were taken.

Many inferences may be made on the basis of the somewhat complex patterns found in these percentage plots and the derived statistics. At present we are concerned with the contribution made by knowing the student's level of self-esteem, and not with reaffirming the already-established findings that

Figure 26—Global self-esteem and desire for education, by social class, verbal ability, and parental aspirations.

( ) indicates that base for percentage is less than 10

% INDICATING A DESIRE TO OBTAIN A B.A. OR GO ON

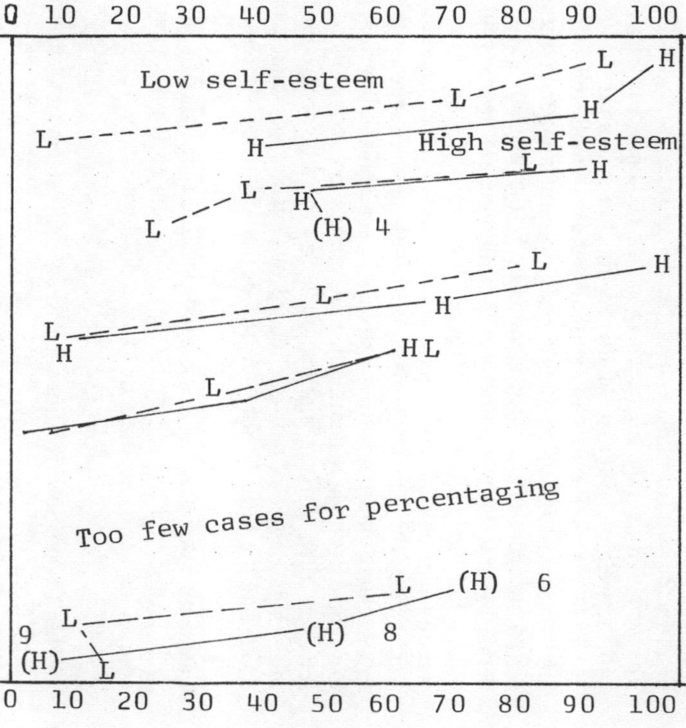

Low self-esteem

High self-esteem

Too few cases for percentaging

	(1) Social Class	(2) Verbal Ability	(3) Parental Aspirations	(4) E	(5) D	(6) N
18	Middle	+	High	+.10	+.06**	244
17	Middle	+	Medium	+.21	+.11	128
16	Middle	+	Low	+.28	+.16*	66
15	Middle	-	H	+.12	+.02	56
14	Middle	-	M	+.08	+.10	59
13	Middle	-	L	(+.24)	-.07	51
12	Working	+	H	+.18	+.11*	140
11	Working	+	M	+.20	+.13	108
10	Working	+	L	+.02	+.05	111
9	Working	-	H	+.00	+.02	78
8	Working	-	M	+.05	+.06	114
7	Working	-	L	-.08	-.009	149
6	Lower	+	H		+.47	8
5	Lower	+	M		+.52	14
4	Lower	+	L		+.46	19
3	Lower	-	H	(+.04)	+.09	34
2	Lower	-	M	(+.33)	+.20	51
1	Lower	-	L	(-.08)	-.03	97

0 10 20 30 40 50 60 70 80 90 100

$\overline{E} = +.094$ $\overline{D} = +.075$

social class, verbal ability, and parental aspiration all have substantial effects on level of educational aspiration (thus producing the regular left-to-right configuration of level of aspiration as one reads up the table). It should be pointed out that base n's are small in the high self-esteem category in four of the groups (numbers 1, 2, 3, & 13), and were so small in the lower-class groups higher in verbal ability (4, 5 & 6) that no percentaging could be relied upon. Even with small numbers of cases in the tables, the D measure still gives a fairly good indication of the asymmetric relation between self-esteem and educational aspiration, independent of social class, verbal ability, and parental aspiration.

First and most important, the predicted positive relation between self-esteem and educational aspiration holds up even after introduction of the three-factor control in 15 out of the 18 groups ($p = .004$ by the sign test). The weighted average of the 18 D values (column 5 in Figure 26) is +.075, and the weighted average of the 15 Epsilons (column 4) is +.094. Only 3 of the D values are negative; these are very small and all are among those not subjected to their parents' urging: group number 1, the lower-class, less verbal students (D = —.03); number 7, the working-class, less verbal students (—.009); and number 13, the middle-class, less verbal students (—.07 in the full table despite the rather high rate of aspiration among the few respondents high in self-esteem, because those rated "medium" in self-esteem were quite low). Such remarkable consistency suggests that regardless of social class, children with relatively less verbal skill whose parents do not urge them to high educational achievement are not driven, either by themselves or their parents, hard enough toward advanced education for even a fairly high degree of self-confidence or sense of personal worth to overcome these deficits. Furthermore (to the degree that these extremely small negative D's reflect even a slight negative relationship in the population from which this sample was drawn), it is even possible that some of these students, low in academic ability but highest in self-esteem, will turn away from long-term courses of action leading to extended education as representing unauthentic lifestyles.

The 15 positive relations between self-esteem and desire for education range from the very tiny +.02 to a somewhat more substantial +.16* in the groups with reasonable numbers of cases. The three categories of lower-class, relatively more verbal students (4, 5, & 6) show much higher relationships than do any of the others (+.46, +.52, and +.47). That these strong relations between self-esteem and aspiration occur only among verbally skilled students in the most disadvantaged situation suggests that self-esteem may be especially important in the more verbal who are experiencing *incongruous* components of social structure and social influence. This interpretation is supported by the finding that among middle-class students who rank in the high half of the range of verbal ability, self-esteem is most strongly related to educational aspiration among those whose parents entertain relatively low aspirations for them (D = +.16*, as against +.11 and +.06** among the students classified under "medium" and high parental aspiration, respectively). The interpretation in terms of incongruity just mentioned leads to the expectation that among working-class students self-esteem is most strongly related to educational aspiration in those cases where at least one parent urges the student to high educational achievement. The patterns seen in groups 10, 11, and 12 bear out this inference: D = +.13 and +.11* in the groups classified by medium, and high parental aspiration, respectively, as against +.02 where parental aspirations are low. These outcomes, together with the fact that self-esteem is related to educational aspiration more strongly among those whose measured verbal ability is high than among those who score lower, suggest that self-esteem may exert a multiplier effect, giving confidence and a sense of appropriateness to students who presumably have the ability to compete in college and graduate school.

VI

VI. A MODEL ASSESSING THE PROPOSED JOINT IMPACT OF SOCIAL STRUCTURE, FAMILY, ABILITY, AND SELF-CONCEPTION ON ORIENTATION TO ACHIEVEMENT

Summary of the individually tested relationships

The preceding analysis of specific hypothesized relations between pairs of variables was carried out by the strategy of controlling other factors by separating the cases according to their position on one, two, or even three additional variables. This procedure requires detailed inspection of the direction and magnitude of many different sub-relations, some of which were assessed from very small numbers of cases where some intersection of the several control variables was sparsely populated in our sample of 1684 ninth-graders in the urban Northeast. While producing a complex set of comparisons, this technique does treat the variables as ordered sets of two, three, or four categories and, further, it expresses the resulting sub-relations in terms of cross-tabulations and derived measures of association or tests of insignificance that make relatively weak assumptions about levels of measurement and forms of the underlying distributions. In spite of the fact that a lengthy and involved presentation of findings is thereby made necessary, these features of controlled cross-tabulation analysis do allow the reader to see clearly what is going on and at the same time they inspire his confidence in the substantive findings and in the inferences. These inferences (of which interpretations were given earlier) will now be reviewed before we attempt to synthesize them in a more comprehensive model.

On the basis, therefore, of the foregoing controlled cross-tabulation, the major outcomes of this study may be summarized in the following generalizations:

1. As hypothesized, black students are more often than white found in broken or "weak-male" families (D = +.23***). Moreover, black lower-class students are more likely than their white counterparts to be living with their mothers only (44% as compared to 29% of the whites).

2. *Contrary* to hypothesis, broken or "weak-male" families are *not* appreciably more common in the working class than in the middle class; in fact, to a slight degree the reverse is true among blacks (25% to 31%).

3. *Contrary* to hypothesis, white children do *not* more frequently than black children report that their parents urge them to high achievement in school and to go on to college. In fact, in the lower and working class, the black parents are somewhat *more* often reported to do this kind of urging.

4. As hypothesized, the higher the social class, the higher the level of reported urging by parents toward educational achievement (D = +.22*** among blacks, +.28*** among whites).

5. As hypothesized, white students are found to have higher measured verbal ability than black students (D = +.40*** over-all; +.13** in the lower class; +.30*** in the working class; and +.50*** in the middle class).

6. As hypothesized, social class is directly related to measured verbal ability (D = +.13*** among blacks, and +.30*** among whites).

7. As hypothesized, black students generally have somewhat less favorable self-conceptions than do whites. The findings were in the predicted direction in five out of the six non-independent comparisons (on the sense of competence the races scored essentially the same), but only with the indices of self-rated brightness (D = +.14***), self-determination (D = +.15***), and global self-esteem (D = +.10***), were the relations of any appreciable magnitude. (A problem presented by this finding will be discussed later.)

8. As hypothesized, social class is directly related to favorability of self-conception, across all six dimensions, but with quite small degrees of association (D = +.07** with basic self-acceptance, +.18*** with global self-esteem, +.20*** with self-perceived brightness, and +.13*** with the sense of self-determination).

9. As hypothesized, black students are *more* likely to *desire* advanced education (in five out of six race-and-class comparisons, but with magnitudes of only —.17** or less); but *less* likely to *expect* to enter an occupation with high status, especially in the middle class (D = +.16**).

10. As hypothesized, social class is directly related to both desire for education (+.19*** among blacks, +.29*** among whites), and occupational expectation (+.20*** among blacks, +.26*** among whites). The same pattern appears in the relationship between actual school performance and enrollment in the college preparatory course.

INDEPENDENT OF THE FOREGOING RELATIONSHIPS CONCERNING RACE AND SOCIAL CLASS:

11. As hypothesized, family role structure is associated, although weakly, with the level of parental educational aspiration in all six of the race-and-class comparisons, with substantial non-linearity in some.

12. As hypothesized, family role structure is associated with measured verbal ability, more strongly among white students (+.25***) than among blacks (+.10*). More problematic is the fact that the class relations take different forms in the two racial groups, and the various family configurations seem to have different meanings in different race-and-class situations. One pattern is clear: in all cases, except the middle-class blacks, the home in which both parents are present but the father is not working has a lower proportion of students who fall in the top half of the range of measured ability than is the case in the corresponding matriarchy group.

13. As hypothesized, family role structure is associated with the student's self-conception, across all the dimensions except the index of over-all competence. The particular values (D = +.06 for basic self-acceptance, +.18** for self-rated brightness, +.08 for academic competence, +.11*** for the sense of self-determination, and +.12** for global self-esteem) were seen to be quite conservative assessments. They held up fairly well as the joint race-and-class controls were introduced, social class having greater conditioning effect than race. Most interesting is the fact that, as predicted, the "weak-male" configuration is associated with higher rates of self-disparagement than is the matriarchy—even higher occasionally than the "neither-parent-present" configuration. The "strong-male" and matriarchy patterns are about equal in their low frequencies of self-rejection, while the "weak-male" and "neither-parent-present" patterns tend to substantially higher rates of self-rejection.

14. As hypothesized, family role structure is associated with educational and occupational aspirations, in patterns very similar to those with self-conception, but somewhat weaker in magnitude. Once again, the relations are stronger among whites than among blacks. When social class is introduced as a control, it is found that the "weak-

male" and "strong-male" patterns are similar except among working- and lower-class whites. Children from the matriarchy more often express high occupational expectation, and in the "weak-male" configuration are found lower proportions of high aspiration.

15. As hypothesized, these data show that the higher the student's measured verbal ability, the higher his aspiration. This relation is consistent and strong (appearing in all of the sub-group comparisons, with a minimum association of D = +.18** and a grand average over all types of aspiration of +.25***). The form of the relation is invariant between the races and across the social classes in the case of whites, but it grows progressively stronger with increasing class level among blacks (+.12*, +.22** and +.37***).

16. As hypothesized, the higher the student's measured verbal ability, the more favorable his self-conceptions. The original correlations of +.27** for blacks and +.36** for whites remain quite substantial even when recomputed as a second-order partial correlation that takes into account the student's race and social class—in which the relation between verbal ability and self-esteem comes out as +.24** among blacks and +.32*** among whites.

17. As hypothesized, the higher the student's measured verbal ability, the higher his parents' aspiration regarding his educational achievement. The over-all relationship (weighted average D = +.23) holds up regardless of race, and again is stronger in the higher social classes (—.06 and +.14 in lower-, +.19* and +.24*** in working-, and +.29** and +.34*** in middle-class black and white students).

18. As hypothesized, the higher the reported parental aspiration toward educational achievement, the higher the student's own reported aspirations. Even after race and class are controlled, the predicted relation between parental aspiration and how good a student the respondent says he wants to be is maintained near the original level (Tau C = +.54***; ranging from +.41*** to +.59*** in the sub-groups). Almost as robust is the relation with expressed desire to obtain at least a B.A. (over-all Tau C = +.63***; spreading in the sub-groups from +.33*** to +.66***). Weakest is the relation of parental aspiration to occupational expectation (Tau C = +.20***; rising to +.25*** among middle-class whites, but dropping to +.04 among lower-class whites). In all, 16 of the 18 instances show the predicted relation as persisting, with significant and strong values.

19. As hypothesized, the higher the level of reported parental aspirations, the more favorable the student's self-conceptions. The original small-to-moderate associations (ranging from D = +.11*** with basic self-acceptance to a high of +.29*** with self-rated brightness, a value of +.25*** with global self-esteem) are maintained quite well even after social class and objectively measured verbal

ability are controlled. The relation is much stronger among the brighter students from disadvantaged backgrounds.

INDEPENDENT OF ALL THE PRECEDING RELATIONS:

20. As hypothesized, the more favorable the self-conception, the higher the aspiration. The average zero-order correlations among all the dimensions of self-conception and those of aspiration fall generally between r = +.14** and +.36,** the non-academic competencies being more closely associated with aspiration than is basic self-acceptance. When race and social class are controls on the relationships of global self-esteem to both educational and occupational aspirations, the resulting curves are positive in all cases and moderately strong in many (ranging from +.07 among lower-class blacks to +.35*** among middle-class blacks), and of extraordinary linearity in 9 of the 12 instances. Race is much less important as a conditioning factor than are social class, parental aspiration, and measured verbal ability. Even with all these factors controlled, self-esteem still stands in positive relation with educational aspiration in 15 of the 18 sub-groups, with a weighted average D value of +.075. The highest values appear where there is some incongruity among social structure, social influence and the components of individual ability. Here self-esteem may serve as a multiplier or accelerator factor.

In short, 18 of the 20 original hypotheses were confirmed by the analysis of our data within the specified controls and within the limits of this particular sample. Although the magnitudes of the observed relationships were often quite weak, statistical levels of confidence were in almost all cases well in excess of conventional values. Now it becomes the task of analysis to reassemble these individual relationships into the beginning of a more comprehensive model of the process by which adolescent orientation to achievement is developed.

Path analysis, theory building and empirical display

A number of mathematically sophisticated research workers have in recent years imported into the sociological literature a very powerful form of multivariate statistical analysis that was long ago developed in genetics and economics (Blalock, 1964; Duncan, 1966; Blau and Duncan, 1967; Sewell and Shah, 1967, 1968; Elder, 1968; Blalock, 1969; Land, 1969). This general method, usually called path analysis, is intended to aid in assessing, at least roughly, the estimated differential effects (both direct and indirect) of a set of independent and intervening variables on one or more dependent variables, as all are mutually interrelated in a specifically organized theoretical model that is assumed to be selectively isomorphic with an actual empirical causal system operating on the parent population. Path analysis includes procedures intended to assess the total amount of presumed "recursive" (asymmetric, one-way) "causal effect" or determination produced by each of the independent and intervening variables. That is, path analysis seeks to establish the amount of change in a "dependent" variable that would be associated with one unit of change in one or more of the "determining" variables, while all the others are held constant. Path analysis also includes measures of the total effect produced by the entire set of variables in the system, and of the "residual" effects that unmeasured variables exert on each of the intervening and dependent variables.

Path analysis is logically related to partial correlation, multiple regression, and factor analysis, but possesses unique advantages in that its basic analytic paradigm is the kind of hypothesized theoretical model that social scientists usually wish to construct and test. It involves solution of a set of structural equations and equations of path estimation into which the inputs are the complete set of zero-order Pearsonian correlation coefficients among all the variables, plus a specified set of presumed causal orderings. The principal outcomes are a set of path coefficients (standardized beta weights) in the appropriate multiple regression analyses; but if even one path is deleted by the investigator, the calculation of the path coefficients also involves the asserted structure of interrelations of the independent and intervening variable with each other as well as with the dependent variables of primary interest. (See the technical paper, "A new definition of 'path coefficient,'" by Fred Bookstein, 1970).

In the conventional representation of a proposed causal model as a path diagram, those variables assumed to be independent are arrayed at the left and then connected by arrows representing "causal paths" to intervening variables in the center. Then additional arrows are drawn to the presumed "outcome" or dependent variable(s) at the right. The arrows carry the appropriate estimated path coefficient (p), which generally will range from +1.000 to —1.000 (although they can be larger under special circumstances) and which are usually given in three decimal places to distinguish them from simple zero-order Pearsonian correlation coefficients.

The relations between the independent variables are treated as unanalyzed and are represented in the diagram by a double-headed curved arrow bearing their simple correlation coefficient. Short vertical arrows leading to each intervening and dependent variable represent the magnitude of the "residual" of each, or the effects on each of all other factors not explicitly included in the theoretical model. Finally, each dependent variable and each intervening variable may be associated with a "coefficient of multiple determination" (MR^2), which is the square of the relevant multiple regression coefficient. This MR^2 gives the proportion of that variable's variance that is "explained" by reference to all the variables from which arrows lead into it. This coefficient of multiple determination is also used in calculating the value of the residual for each variable, by the formula $\sqrt{1\text{-}MR^2}$.

The path coefficient as a measure of direct effect—Each path coefficient estimates the direct effect of one variable on another to the right of it in the diagram. That is, p is an estimate of the fraction of the standard deviation of the dependent variable (with the appropriate sign) for which the designated independent or intervening variable is "directly responsible"—by which is meant the average change in the dependent variable that would presumably occur if the determining factor were varied by one standard deviation in each data case while all other variables (including residual variables) were held constant (paraphrased from Land, 1969:10).

Mediated indirect effects and total effects—One of the tenets of this form of analysis is that the total relation of one variable (X_1) with another (X_2), estimated by the simple correlation coefficient (r_{21}), is composed of the direct effect p_{21}, plus the sum of the mediated or indirect effects of X_1 on X_2 via the intervening variables, plus the sum of the "spurious" effects due to mutual correlation of both X_1 and X_2 with antecedent and co-equal variables. The aggregate strength of the indirect paths from one variable to another is obtained by multiplying the path coefficients on the relevant arrows, and then summing these products to yield the total mediated effect. This principle provides one of the advantages that path analysis has over multiple regression: a change in a "determining variable" may have a very small direct effect on the outcome variable (thus yielding a small value of p, and hence of the analogous beta weight in the regression analysis). Yet it may also operate in an indirect manner through one or more intervening variables, and thus have a large total postulated causal effect (which would have no measure in the regression analysis). Conversely, in path analysis a substantial zero-order correlation ("total effect") may be shown to be largely "spurious" if the potency of determination is almost exclusively through the "accidental" association of the intervening variable with one or more strongly effective "antecedents."

In summary, path analysis is a form of multivariate analysis that is designed to use a theoretically specified structure of presumed asymmetric causal relations among a set of measured variables, together with their intercorrelations as empirically obtained in a sample, in order to calculate a set of path coefficients, estimations of residuals, and coefficients of multiple determination with which to estimate the relative direct and indirect effects that changes in the independent and intervening variables would be expected to have on the dependent variable in the population and settings that the sample is held to represent.

Assumptions—The mathematical logic of path analysis requires, first, that the investigator assume each of the variables is either measured at the interval level or is a true point dichotomy. However, as Land and others have pointed out (*ibid.*, pp. 33-34), relatively little important error will be introduced in most instances if this assumption is sufficiently relaxed to permit the use of variables that are measured in what might best be termed "partially interval" form, such as produced by the construction of indexes or scaling procedures that do result in a continuous series of relatively finely divided scores even though there is no actual unit of measure to provide an invariant interval. Second, the investigator must assume that the variables in the model are related to each other in a linear, additive fashion, at least within the ranges of values obtained in the sample. Change in one variable is assumed to be a linear (additive) function of change in one or more of the other variables, such as ($X = aY + bZ + e$), where e is a residual error term and where a

and *b* are the path coefficients or weights attached to the Y and Z variables.

These assumptions of interval measurement and linear additivity are in no way different from those required by the use of any correlation or regression procedure; path analysis does, however, require the further assumption that the variables are connected in an *asymmetric* causal relation. This assumption, of course, is hazardous, given the present state of existing sociological knowledge, but some ground for particular assertions can be found in knowledge about time-order relationships, in previous experimental research, or simply in the theoretical predisposition of the investigator (*ibid.,* p. 34). There are some discussions of methods of path analysis for use where causal ordering is cloudy or where there is rapid interaction between dependent variables (e.g., Blalock, 1964:ch. 2), but as in the case of the suggestions sometimes made to use path analysis to test the relative merits of different arrangements of the variables in the causal models (ibid., ch.3; Land, ibid., pp. 34-36), the issues are by no means yet resolved. The absorbing quality of path analysis even in its present form is that it challenges the investigator to put his theory where his data are. A further assumption of path analysis is that the residuals of the dependent variables are uncorrelated with each other and with the scores on the independent variables. It is actually this assumption which makes possible a determinant solution of the simultaneous equations involved in the analysis, and which is at the mathematical heart of the computer program that was used to carry out the analysis reported below.*

Problems of path analysis—For some time after the introduction of a new and seemingly very powerful procedure, there tends to be a good deal of enthusiasm but little rigorous criticism. Perhaps one of the most thorough expositions of path analysis yet published is that by Heise (1969), who discusses many of the difficulties associated with the low reliability of measurement, non-linear relations, correlated residuals, and the like. His thoughful review makes it clear that the assumptions may be weakened with little serious error as long as the investigator remembers that the path coefficients are only rough estimates, and does not begin to believe that the resulting path diagrams present some kind of ultimate and exact specification of causal priorities and magnitudes. Further, path analysis can be very useful in contradicting previously held theories about the relative effectiveness of determining factors and in parsimoniously displaying existing theoretical formula-

---

* A general purpose path analysis program called PATHCO was developed under the author's guidance by Fred Bookstein, a graduate student in sociology in Harvard's Department of Social Relations, who has an extensive background in both mathematics and computer programming, with the gratefully acknowledged support of the National Institute of Mental Health's Grant No. 12132, by the Laboratory of Social Relations, and by the Harvard Computing Center. PATHCO is designed to solve the necessary equations by a least-squares method of minimizing the correlation of each residual with every other variable. Although logically and algebraically consistent with other procedures described in the literature, this method has the advantage of using more of the information in the theoretically structured diagram. On the theoretical and computational strategy, see the paper by Bookstein (1970). Information on the PATHCO program in the FORTRAN language for use at other computing facilities may be secured from the Social Relations Computing Facility, 13th floor, William James Hall, Harvard University, Cambridge, Massachusetts, 02138.

tions so that additional variables can be suggested. Heise put the conclusion well (ibid., p. 69):

> Path analysis and causal inference procedures invite a critical review precisely because they are so powerful and are such distinct advances over previous methods of causal analysis and theory testing. To a large degree, it is only with the appearance of these tools in sociology that we know how cautious we must be in making causal inferences from cross-sectional data. Old techniques of tabular elaboration, partial correlations, and stepwise regressions all involve similar assumptions and these old techniques now seem almost archaic in comparison with the techniques discussed above.
>
> Path diagrams and path analysis force awareness of the ambiguities in sociological thinking, and this alone justifies their usage. In addition, path analysis provides a powerful, meaningful approach to analyzing causal relations and correlations, and it is assured of wide acceptance as a tool for abstract analysis.

A path analysis of the causal relations proposed in the present theoretical model

The path analysis summarized in Figures 27A and B has been constructed as a method of integrating the structure of propositions that has been the organizing framework of this entire analysis, and as a more comprehensive and powerful procedure for recasting the empirical tests of the hypotheses. The path diagrams were prepared separately to correct the oversampling of black students, and to provide a comparative context for evaluating path analysis itself.

The variables of social class and family structure are defined in the same manner as in the preceding cross-tabular analyses, while parental educational aspiration appears with its original 5 levels, running from "very low" to "very high." The measured verbal ability variable is in the original point scores (which have approximately 100 values), and the index of global self-esteem is in its original range of scores from 0 to 20. Desire for education, in its 6-point form, was selected because of all the aspirations it is the one of greatest importance in this kind of analysis of mobility as found in the sociological literature; it is also of greatest immediate significance to the students in the sample.

Path analysis of some factors shaping desire for education among white students

Because of the oversampling of black students, the path analysis diagrams must be presented separately for each race. Figures 27A and B give, for each race, the direct path coefficients of each of the hypothesized paths in the causal model. In this kind of complete model, where all the arrows are entered, the path coefficients are equal to regular standardized beta weights from the appropriate series of multiple regressions. In general, these coefficients substantiate the conclusions presented at the beginning of this section. The graphically displayed path diagram also renders the whole system more

Figure 27A—Path analysis of the proposed theoretical model, blacks only.

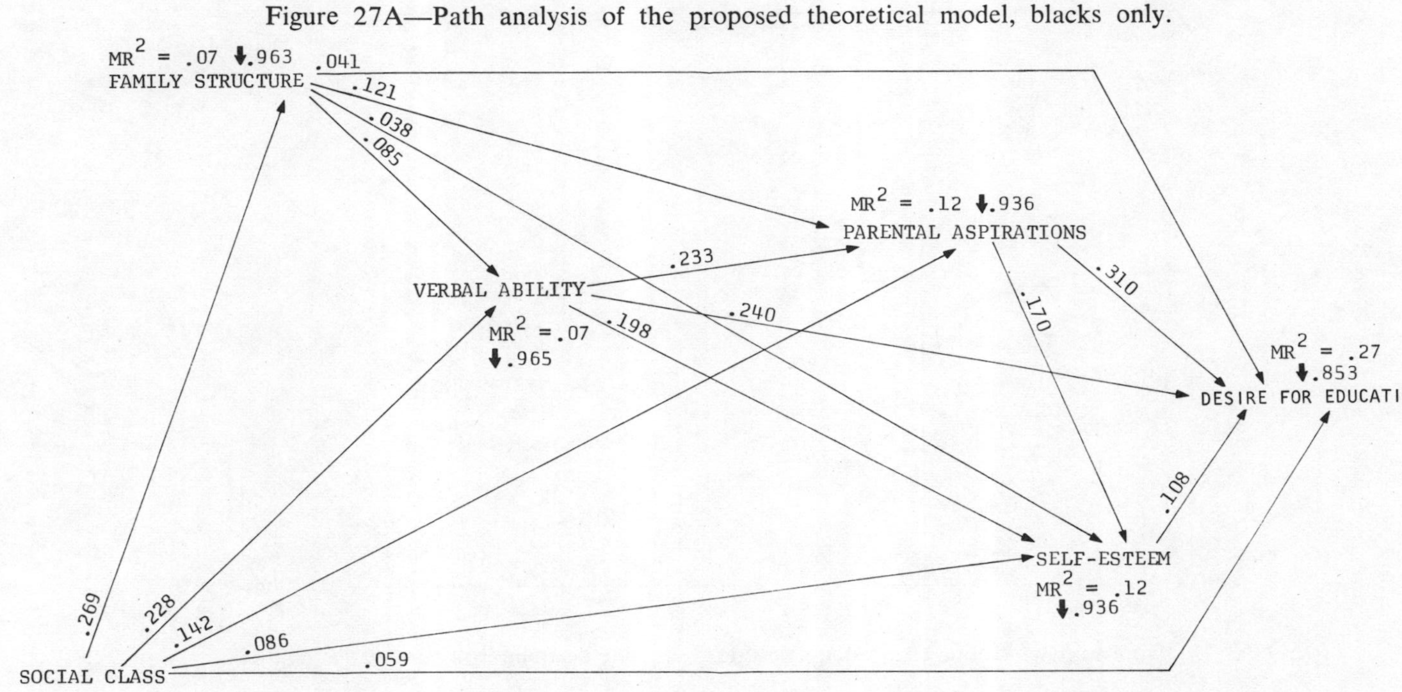

Figure 27B—Path analysis of the proposed theoretical model, whites only.

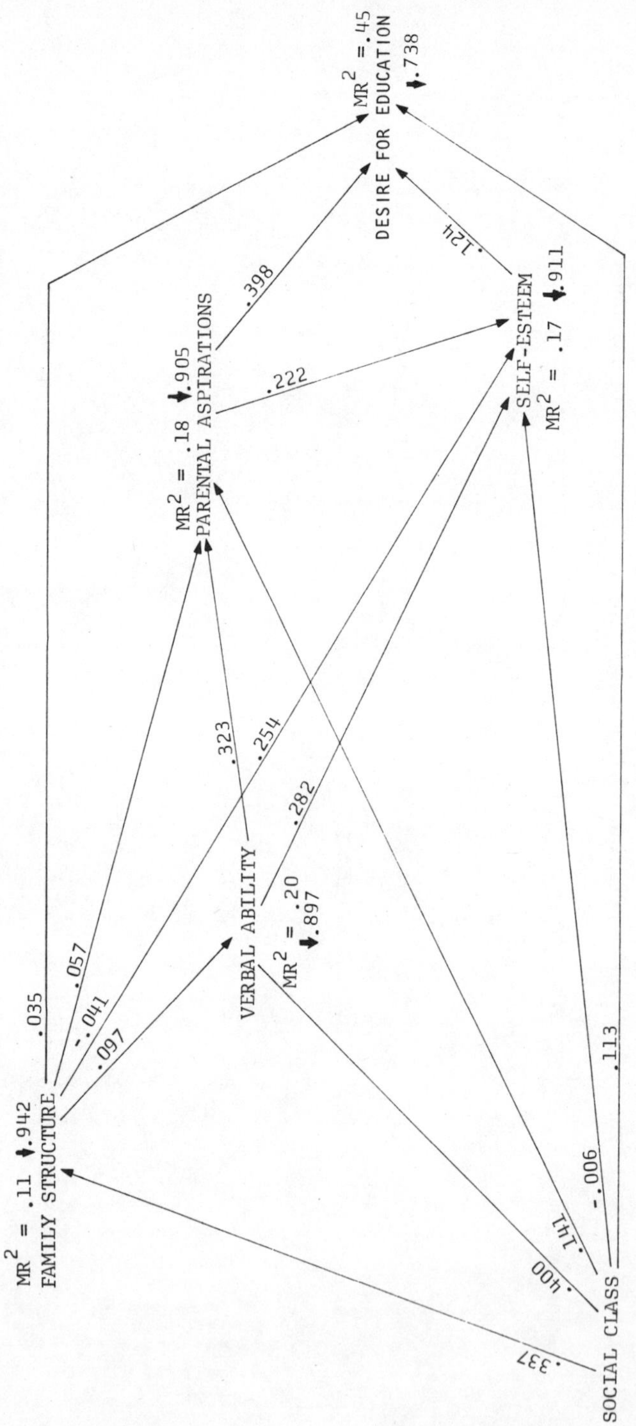

MR^2 = .11 ↓.942
FAMILY STRUCTURE

MR^2 = .18 ↓.905
PARENTAL ASPIRATIONS

VERBAL ABILITY
MR^2 = .20
↓.897

MR^2 = .45
DESIRE FOR EDUCATION
↓.738

SELF-ESTEEM
MR^2 = .17 ↓.911

SOCIAL CLASS

.035
.057
-.041
.097
.323
.254
.282
.222
.398
.124
.337
.400
.141
-.006
.113

comprehensible and facilitates the detection of the most problematic relationships. Later on, simplified models from which the weakest and least important paths have been removed will be compared, but before that it will be useful to examine the relative postulated causal effects of each of the major variables on desire for education, first among the white students, as shown in the left-hand column of Figure 28B.

Among the white students (Figures 27B and 28B), the entire set of five variables predicts desire for education at a level of $MR^2 = .45$ (which thus gives a regular multiple correlation coefficient of over $+.67$). This means that 45% of the variance in desire for education has been accounted for by reference to the entire set of independent and intervening variables at the left-hand center of Figure 27B. Although an MR^2 of .45 does mean that some 55% of the variance in desire for education is left unaccounted for, the 45% that has been explained is much higher than the from 20 to 25% that has usually been explained in research that does not include parental aspiration, family structure, or self-conception as hypothesized causal factors (cf. Sewell and Shah, 1967, 1968).

Comparison of the variables according to their total postulated causal effects on desire for education among the white students (portrayed as vertical height in the left-hand column of Figure 28B), shows that verbal ability and reported parental aspiration have essentially identical and very strong effects: .426 and .425. For the sake of clarity, the links from parental aspiration will be discussed first. The direct path of .398 tying parental aspiration to desire for education is strongest in the entire diagram; very little indirect mediated effect is gained by the link through self-esteem ($.222 \times .124 = .027$). By means of the PATHCO computer program, which also computes values of suprious effects of one variable on another traceable to their mutual relations to antecedent variables, the total relation of the effects of parental aspiration on educational aspiration is shown to have been composed of the obtained .425 in total postulated causal effects, plus .154 in spurious effects (.034 via social class, .005 via family economic role structure, and .115 via verbal ability). In cases such as this, where all the possible causal paths have been included in the model, the sum of the total postulated causal effects of parental aspiration on desire for education (.425) and the obtained spurious effects (.154) exactly equals the original zero-order correlation between the two variables (.79). As will be seen later, if one or more of the possible causal paths were to be deleted from the model for theoretical reasons or in the interest of clarity, the sums of the obtained total postulated causal effects (direct and mediated) plus the obtained values of the spurious effects through antecedent variables would not exactly equal the original correlations. Methods are currently being devised for using these discrepancies to evaluate the relative plausibility of various models to that this form of path analysis can be used in testing alternative hypotheses concerning causal order and intervening connections among a set of variables.

Parental educational aspiration has the largest of all the direct paths to desire for education (.398), thus strongly supporting hypothesis 18. Also, the path of .222 from parents' aspiration to self-esteem lends credence to

Figures 28A and 28B—The ranking of contributing variables to desire for education and occupational expectation among black and white students.

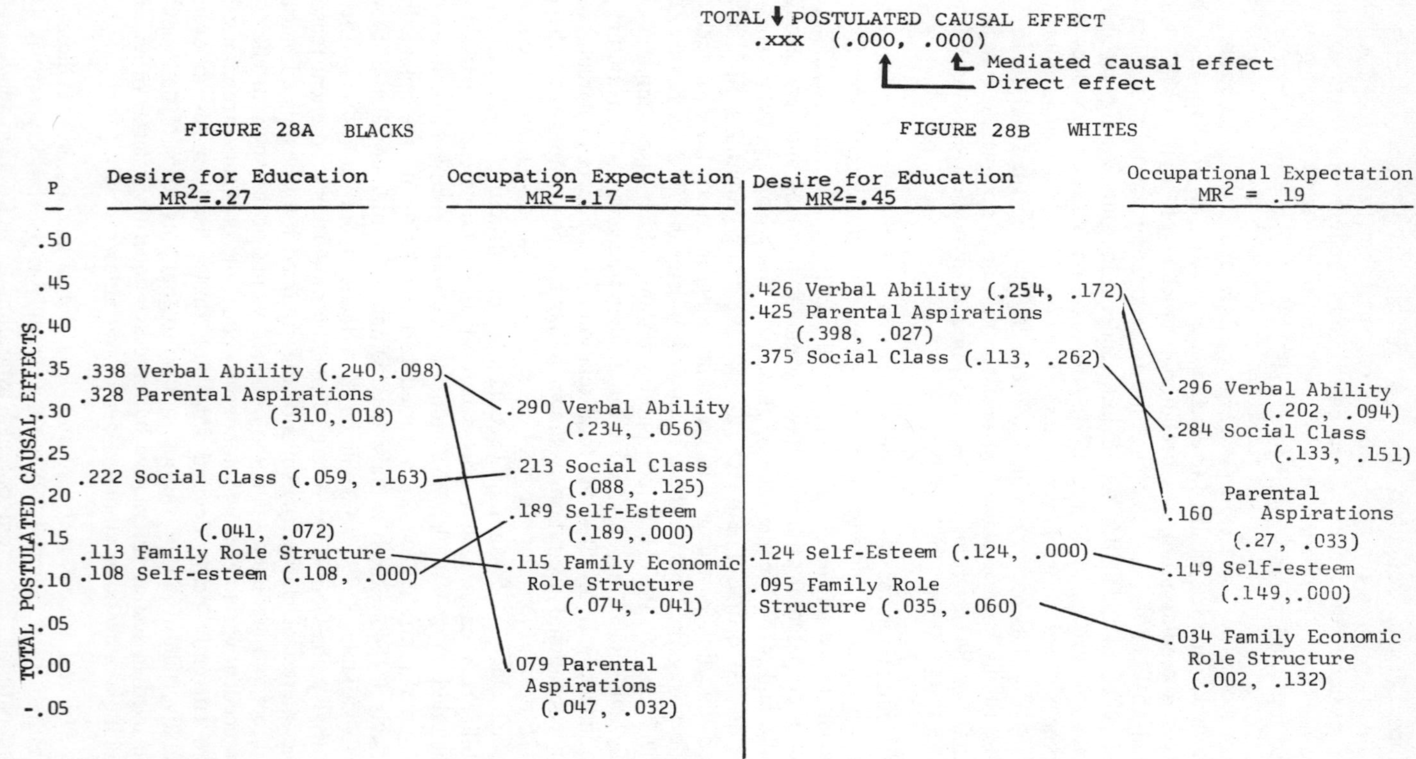

hypothesis 19, and this value is very close to that of the average of the Somers' D's ($\overline{D} = .18$) computed from the cross-tabulations produced when social class and verbal ability were controlled in the relations between parents' educational aspiration and the students' own desire for education. The value of MR^2 for parental aspiration shows that only some 18% of its variance has been accounted for by the combination of social class, family structure and verbal ability; of these, verbal ability is by far the most important (as shown by the direct path of .323). Since this variable, parental educational aspiration, is of such potency in the developing model of adolescent orientation to achievement, it would be good to know what kinds of other factors help to establish its level in particular cases. Because it is an attitudinal rather than a structural factor, it is quite possible that any number of persuasive programs might encourage parents to visualize college or even an advanced degree as part of their children's future and to urge them toward those goals. Yet this alone would leave untouched the very severe problems of making elementary, secondary, and advanced education sufficiently rewarding and meaningful, and of providing open occupational career structures so that the increased parental pressure would do more than simply inculcate senseless competitiveness, but rather would have a valid purpose.

Measured verbal ability has a fairly large direct path to desire for education among these white students (.254), thus giving support to hypothesis 15. Of course, the reader should be aware that this word "direct" in path analysis means only "not mediated by any of the variables specified in this particular diagrammed theoretical model." Unknown portions of this influence are in fact mediated by such factors as the student's interpretations of the meaning of his long history of school grades, his friends' comments on how smart they think he is, his teachers' advice and encouragement in decisions concerning educational problems, and a host of other variables. The size of this "direct" path thus is an open invitation to improve the scope and subtlety of future research. Verbal ability's path to self-esteem is even stronger than to educational aspiration (.282) supporting hypothesis 16, and still more substantial is the direct path from verbal ability to parental aspiration (.323), thereby validating the reasoning behind hypothesis 17.

The MR^2 associated with measured verbal ability indicates that approximately 20% of its variance is accounted for by the combination of social class, (direct path of .400) and the rough variable of family structure (.097); but of course, one would also want to know the additional effects of sibling position, ethnic culture, exposure to the media, patterns of peer interaction, early childhood or even prenatal nutrition, differential experiences of school and of socialization and so on. In any case, the very sizable direct and indirect effects of measured verbal ability on desire for education make it quite clear that this dimension should be included in any attempt to formulate a reasonably comprehensive model of the processes of adolescent orientation to achievement.

Social class is slightly less strong as a determinant of educational aspiration among the white students (.375 total; .113 direct, and .262 indirect). This fairly large indirect link is composed mainly of a .170 path through verbal ability, and a .060 path through parental aspiration. The specific nature of this indirect mediation has potentially important policy implications, because some of the more potent intervening factors may be influenced directly through intentional individual and social action, even though social class position itself is extremely resistant to structural alteration. In the present case, social class influences desire for education principally through verbal ability (.170), and also through parental aspiration (.060), with self-esteem and family structure as extremely weak links in the system. This finding suggests that innovations such as community child development centers that can offer children physiological, cognitive-symbolic and interactional stimulation while simultaneously involving the parents in the process of orientation to achievement might well ultimately evoke high educational aspirations in the young. The question then becomes how to make educational institutions and eventual occupational structures support and be worthy of the heightened expectations.

Family role structure as conceptualized and categorized in the present instance is not a good variable for use in a path analysis, since the structural categories are so bound up with social class and have many more meanings than merely their rough ordering on approximation to the cultural ideal of "both parents present with the father employed." In addition, the meanings differ greatly as between the races, as concerning males or females, and in the various social classes. As was noted in the analyses of hypotheses 11 to 14, the family role-structure variable operates in many non-linear ways, and thus we would expect it to have only very weak linear paths to the other variables. Indeed, this is the case: family structure shows only .095 in total postulated causal effect on desire for education (.035 direct, plus .060 indirect). Since all the linear paths from family structure are very weak, the entire variable will be eliminated from the simplified path models presented below.

Self-esteem in the white students has a small but positive direct path to desire for education (.124), which is similar in size to the weighted average of the D values (.075) obtained from the tables in which social class, parental aspiration, and measured verbal ability had been introduced as controls. This path justifies some limited confidence in the positive relation between self-esteem and desire for education asserted in hypothesis 20. However, as was noted earlier, the presence of some non-linearity and the fact that self-esteem seems to operate more vigorously as a multiplier effect where structural and individual characteristics are in some way incongruous should lead to more subtle formulations specifying the exact circumstances in which the proposed influence works in different ways. Even though there are reasonably strong paths to self-esteem from verbal ability (.282) and from parental aspiration (.222), the fact that only 17% of the variance in self-esteem is accounted for by the entire combination of preceding variables indicates that a great many elements are missing from the model that might well be shaping aspiration as well as influencing self-esteem. As I have argued elsewhere (Gordon, 1966, 1968a, 1968c), self-esteem may be based on many components of self-conception rather than solely on those middle-class, male-oriented relations to effective instrumental action: competence and self-determination. Self-perceived body image, ethnic and religious identification, group allegiances, role identifications, interests, status interpretations, interpersonal styles, psychic styles, and the senses of unity and moral worth all may be related to the status level and qualitative character of aspirations, as well as forming bases of self-esteem.

Path analysis of some factors influencing occupational expectation among white students

The right-hand column of Figure 28B gives the relative magnitudes of total postulated causal effect of each of the major factors on the white students' occupational expectation. The value of $MR^2 = .19$ indicates that 19% of the variance in the students' occupational expectation was explained by reference to these independent and intervening variables. This portion, while substantial (corresponding to a regular multiple correlation of just over .43), is considerably smaller than the 45% explained in predicting the desire for education of the same students. The longer time perspective and the vagaries in the requirements for entrance into various occupations doubtless help to account for the poorer predictability of occupational expectation.

However, it is interesting to note that with only one exception the predictors show the same relative ordering in total postulated causal effect on both education and occupation. Among the white students, verbal ability at .296 is most important, .202 being direct, and .094 indirect, about equally through parental aspiration and self-esteem. Social class is next at .294 with .132 direct and the bulk of the .151 indirects through verbal ability (.119). Much less potent is parental aspiration (third at .160 total, down from .425 and second place in the prediction of desire for education. This is not surprising, since the forms of parental aspiration reported concerned education only. At about the same level is the measure of global self-esteem (.149 total, all direct). This was the only variable whose power to predict desire for education (.124) had increased, but the difference is too small to warrant speculation about its meaning. Finally, the economic role structure of the family is shown to exert no appreciable linear effects on occupational expectation (.034 total).

Path analysis of some factors influencing desire for education among black students

The relative order of magnitude of total postulated effect on desire for education among the predictor variables is nearly the same in the case of the black students as in the case of the whites. (Figures 27A and 28A). The verbal ability, parental aspiration and social class variables again occupy the three top positions in total determining power, but their absolute levels are much lower than was found among white students, so that the proportion of variance explained in desire for education among the blacks is 27%, as against 45% among the whites. Again it is suggested that many more structural constraints operate in the educational careers of blacks than of whites.

Measured verbal ability, at a total postulated causal effect of .338, has approximately the same direct effect on desire for education as it has in the case of the whites (.240 as compared to .254), but a much smaller set of indirect effects (.098, almost all through parental aspiration). In addition, verbal ability is less determined by social class than it is in whites (.228 as compared to .400). As to its other outcomes, verbal ability is less strongly related to self-esteem than it is among whites (.198 as compared to .282), and also less strongly related to parental aspiration (.233 as compared to .323). In short, compared with its impact among the white students, the measured verbal ability of the black students is not nearly so closely associated with parental aspiration, self-esteem and perhaps other intervening factors that help to establish the level of desire for education.

Parental aspiration is again on a par with verbal ability in total postulated effect on desire for education (.328), and again the large direct effect (.310) receives no appreciable increment through the indirect link via self-esteem (.018). Parents' aspiration is itself not as well explained among blacks as among whites ($MR^2 = .12$ as compared to .18), mainly because verbal ability is not so strongly predictive of it. In turn, parental aspiration is slightly less strongly connected to self-esteem than is the case among whites (.170) as against .222), and also less strongly predictive of desire for education (.310 as compared to .398). It is quite probable that the aspirations of these black students and their parents contain a greater component of fantasy than is the case with the whites.

Social class has a much smaller total postulated causal effect upon blacks than upon whites (.222 as compared to .375), and the difference is due primarily to the smaller indirect path throuh verbal ability (blacks, .077; as against whites, .170). This reduced indirect link is for the most part a result of the weaker connection of social class to verbal ability (blacks, .228; whites, .400). Evidently, the immense pressure on black families to keep to lower- or working-class occupations overwhelms even parents of children with the highest scores on verbal ability.

Family role structure again shows a very low total effect on educational aspiration (.113), one not appreciably different from that obtained in the white students (.095). Because the direct path to desire for education was .041, and since even the largest path from family structure was only .121 into parental aspiration, this variable will not be used in the simplified model to be presented below. No matter how interesting the detailed interactive effects, when coupled with race and other factors, it bears just too little linear relationship to other major variables to justify inclusion in the developing model of adolescent orientation to achievement.

Self-esteem shows a small but positive direct path of the same magnitude into the educational aspiration of the blacks as of the whites (.108 and .124). Although these are by no means large effects, the fact that they are additional and independent of the effects of social class, verbal ability and parental aspiration should be taken into account in interpreting their importance. Self-esteem is itself not as well explained as it is in the white students (12% blacks, vs. 17% whites), but both figures are so low that they indicate an area ripe for the addition of further variables.

Path analysis of some factors shaping occupational expectation among black students

The ranking of the determinants of occupational expectation among the black students is with one exception very similar to that among the whites, and together these factors account for nearly as much of the variance (17%). Verbal ability is again most important at .290, but with very small indirect effects through parental aspiration and self-esteem (.038 and .018). Social class is once more in second place, but with somewhat less potency (.213 as against .284 among whites). Self-esteem has a larger effect as a predictor of occupational expectation of the black students than it has in any of the other connections: .189, all direct. Among the white students, self-esteem is also more important in predicting occupational expectation (.149) than desire for education (.124), but with black students the gap is much wider (.108 for education; .189 for occupation). The size of this difference permits the tentative interpretation that self-esteem may be more closely related to orientations to achievement that are more remote and more colored by fantasy than by reality.

Family role structure shows one of its very few appreciable effects in shaping the black students' occupational expectations (.115). The direct path of .074 is incremented by three very small indirect paths through verbal ability, parental aspiration and self-esteem, adding up to a minuscule .041. These tiny relations are further justification for dropping family structure as a variable from future models.

The one major difference in the pattern of determination or occupational expectation among the black students as compared to the whites is the position of parental aspiration. To both racial groups, parents' aspiration is much less important in determining occupational expectation than in shaping the desire for education. Among the blacks, this variable drops from second down to last place as compared to third place among the whites—a decline which may be explained by the fact that the blacks already know that education will not admit them to the level of job that would be probable and appropriate, if they were white. Perhaps they see ahead of them a world where access to the routinely provided pathways between institutions is blocked. If so, it would help to account for the unusually great importance of self-esteem in establishing occupational expectation: when regular channels are blocked, the individual must try to make decisions in accord with his senses of personal adequacy, of confidence, and of worth.

Race as a determinant of the other factors

Because the Coleman study intentionally oversampled black students to insure sufficient numbers for analysis and comparison, the foregoing analyses have treated the races separately. The proportion of blacks in the sample was .31 instead of the estimated correct proportion of .096 in the population of urban Northeast ninth graders. The variance of the race variable in the sample is therefore much larger than it should be, and since this variance appears in the denominator of every calculation of the correlation of race with any other variable, all these correlation coefficients are smaller than they should be. Finally, the artificially small correlation coefficients of race with other variables have the effect of depressing and limiting the values of path coefficients calculated from them.

Rather than trying to make elaborate and statistically doubtful adjustments to the lowered correlations or the resulting path coefficients, the regular path coefficients (identical with standardized beta weights) are presented here in order to give the reader some grasp of the way in which race is estimated to be causally connected to particular variables, independent of mutual relations with the other factors. Once again, it should be indicated that these paths are lowered estimates because of the oversampling of black students; in any case the rank order of the effects of race on these variables is probably correctly estimated.

Low estimates of direct paths from race to the other variables:

verbal ability,	.334
social class,	.228
family role structure,	.147
self-esteem,	—.033
desire for education,	—.109
parental aspiration,	—.195

The positive paths indicate that whites tend to score somewhat higher than blacks on the measures of social class, family role structure (supporting hypothesis 1), and verbal ability (supporting hypothesis 5). The negative path of —.195 from race to parental aspiration shows that, *contrary* to hypothesis 3, the white parents are *not* more frequently reported by their children to be urging upon them high achievement in school and eventual attendance at college. This reversal was picked up in the rather cumbersome cross-tabular analysis, and it is gratifying to see that the much more parsimonious procedure of path analysis is capable of exposing and measuring this effect, contrary as it is to prediction. The negative path from race to desire for education (—.109) shows that, as predicted in hypothesis 9, the black students have a stronger desire for education than do the white students. Finally, the very small negative path from race to self-esteem (—.033) leads to the conclusion that hypothesis 7 (which gained the weakest possible support when only social class was controlled in the examination of self-conception in the two races) must be rejected now that we have taken account of family structure, verbal ability, and parental aspiration. The path analysis shows what the cross-tabulations could not be sensitive enough to reveal: after all these relevant factors are controlled, the black students are *not* found lower in self-esteem. As has been demonstrated throughout this analysis, it is measured verbal ability and parental aspiration that make the most difference in shaping self-esteem (direct paths of .280 and .207, respectively, in the total sample). Once these factors are included in the model, race no longer has the predicted effect. Hope is to be gleaned from this finding, since both present verbal ability and parents' concern for education can, in principle, be elevated thereby increasing, at least in theory, the black children's self-esteem.

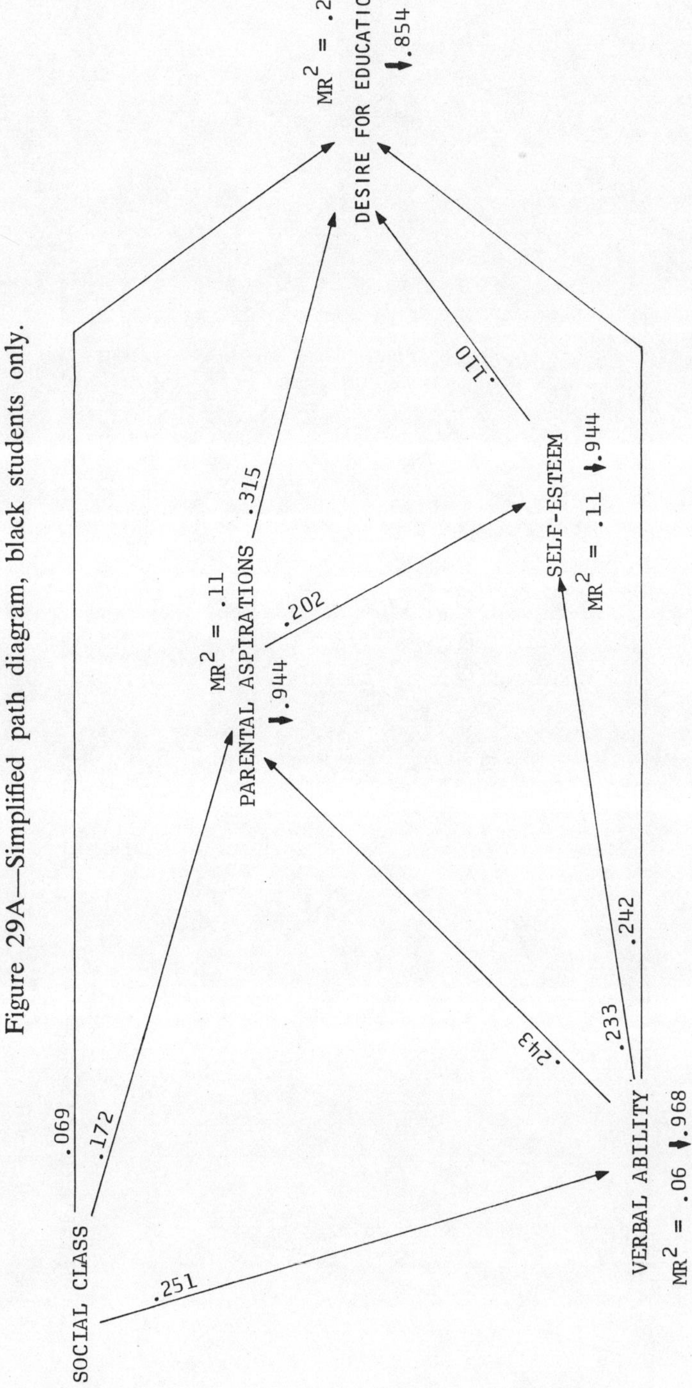

Figure 29A—Simplified path diagram, black students only.

Figure 29B—Simplified path diagram, white students only.

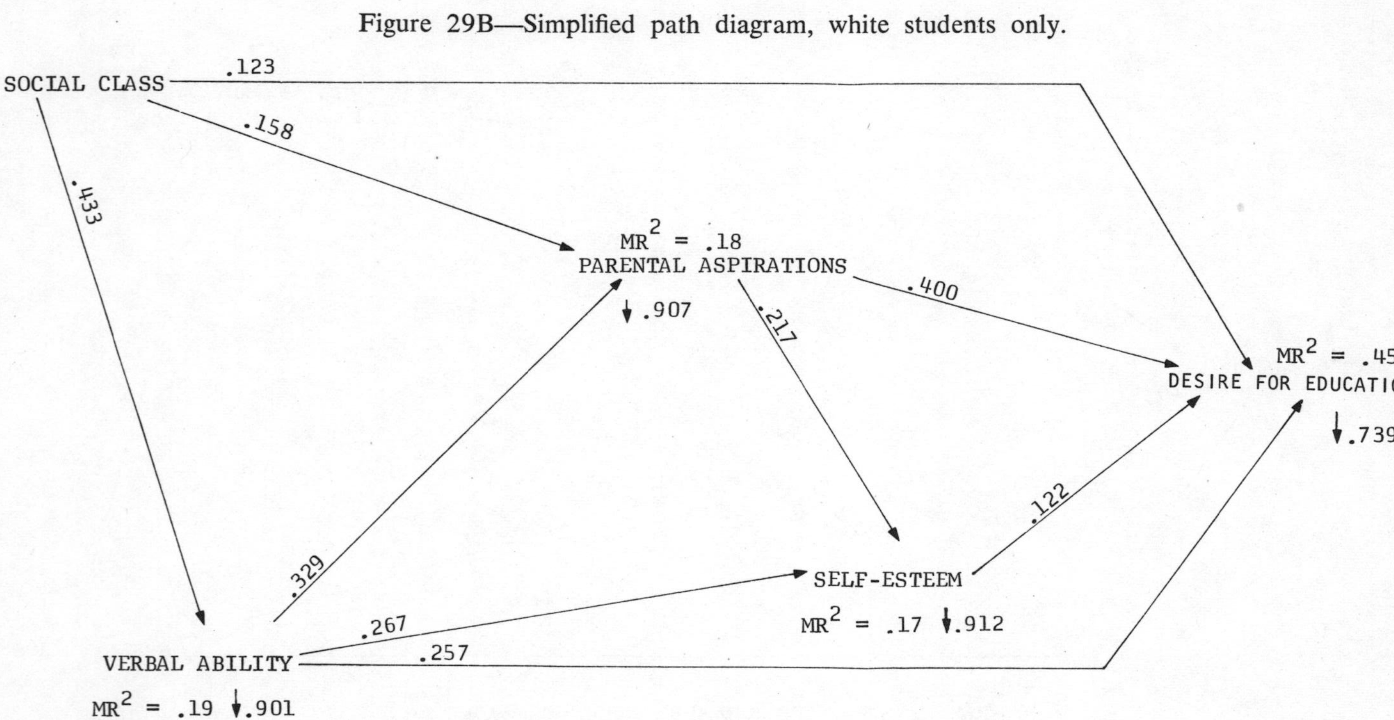

Simplified path diagrams of the model of orientation to achievement

Figures 29A and 29B present the modified path diagrams summarizing estimates of the major one-way causal effects developed from the preceding analysis. They differ from the earlier models in that family structure has been removed as a variable because of its non-linear and non-additive relations with the other variables, and in that the arrow from social class to self-esteem has been deleted because of its insufficient strength (blacks, .086 and whites, —.006). With the removal of even one causal arrow, the path coefficients cease to be exactly equal conceptually and numerically to beta weights.

Among the black students, verbal ability is most important at .349, with .242 direct into desire for education and .107 indirect, mostly through parental aspiration (.082). Parental aspiration is second in causal importance at .337, with only .022 indirect through self-esteem. In third position and considerably lower is social class: .215 via parental aspiration. In last place is self-esteem at .110, all direct. Together, the entire set of variables accounts for 27% of the variance in desire for education in the black students, which leaves plenty of room for other factors to be added in the future.

The total level of determination is much greater among the white students (45%), but the ordering of the causal estimates is identical. Verbal ability here stands at .430 with .257 direct and .173 indirect, mainly through parental aspiration (.140). Parental aspiration is nearly as strong, at .426, having the most potent direct path (.400) and only .026 via self-esteem. Social class is quite close behind at .376, composed of .123 direct, plus .186 through verbal ability and .067 through parental aspiration. Finally, self-esteem has a .122 direct path into desire for education, independent of the effects of the other causal variables and their correlates.

Other possible models

The PATHCO program was used to construct and evaluate other models by the varying of the particular aspiration, the dimension of self-conception and the structure of arrows defining the presumed causal relationships among the intervening variables. Detailed analysis of the differing outcomes is another tale for another time, but it can be said that the models presented in Figures 29 A and B were generally the best according to objective as well as subjective criteria. Ways of using the pattern of direct paths, indirect paths, and correlations of the main residual with the intervening variables are being explored in an effort to discover additional variables that are likely to make strategic contributions to the explanatory power of a model; but this project is not yet sufficiently advanced to be reported.

It may be of some interest to note that global self-esteem has been found to have rather different direct effects on different forms of aspiration. While global self-esteem had direct paths of .108 in the case of blacks and .124 in the case of whites (with $MR^2 = .27$ and .45) to desire for education, the strengths of its connection to the other aspirations were: how good a student the respondent wants to be (.154, .199; $MR^2 = .26$ and .37); high school program (.113, .065; $MR^2 = .21$, 20); and occupational intention (.189,

.199, $MR^2 = .17, .19$). Some increases in predictability are obtained by including a whole new set of variables concerning the specific school context: the student's actual grades to date, the percentage of black and of middle-class students in the school, and the percentage who say that they plan to go to college, and so on. Perhaps enough have been mentioned to illustrate some of the potential power of explanation that path analysis offers to those interested in the construction and empirical testing of causal models of complex processes.

Conclusion

Taken together, the modified path diagrams presented in Figures 29A and B portray in relatively concise and clear form the major postulated causal connections among self-conception, race, ability, and family determinants of adolescent orientation to achievement. Eliminating one entire variable and deleting the weakest paths are distinct steps beyond the mere testing of the hypotheses that had been formulated prior to starting the analysis as the basic theoretical framework. Thus the logic of path analysis allowed assessment of the relative importance of self-esteem and other dimensions of self-conception in comparison with race, social class, verbal ability, family role structure and parental educational aspiration in shaping several forms of aspiration and achievement in this sample of urban Northeast ninth-graders. The most general finding was that self-esteem has a small but consistent independent causal relationship (with path coefficients running approximately from .100 to .190) to desire for education, occupational expectation and other aspirations.

Only with far richer data, a longitudinal research design and far subtler analysis can one hope to explain causation in a process so complex as adolescent orientation to achievement, a process in which social structural, familial, individual, interpersonal, attitudinal, and perceptual elements are interwoven. Previous literature has established social class, mental ability, and parental aspiration as dominating strands in the fabric, and the present analysis has demonstrated that race, the structure of the family, and self-conception are interesting additional threads. It now remains for future work to trace both the deeper tones and the highlights that together brighten the total tapestry.

REFERENCES

Aberle, David F. and Kaspar D. Naegele
1952 "Middle-class fathers' occupational role and attitudes toward children." *American Journal of Orthopsychiatry,* 22(April):366-378.

Adler, Alfred
1956 The Individual Psychology of Alfred Adler: A Systematic Presentation in Selections From His Writings. New York: Harper & Row.

Backman, Carl W., Paul F. Secord, and J. R. Pierce
1963 "Resistance to change in the self-concept as a function of consensus among significant others." *Sociometry,* 26:102-111.
1967 and Paul F. Secord
"The self and role selection." Chapter 28 in Gordon and Gergen (1968).
1968 and Paul F. Secord
A Social Psychological View of Education. New York: Harcourt, Brace & World.

Bakke, E. Wright
1940 Citizens Without Work. New Haven: Yale University Press.

Baldwin, James
1953 Go Tell It On The Mountain. New York: Dell.

Bandura, Albert, Dorothea Ross, and Sheila A. Ross
1963 "A comparative test of the status envy, social power, and secondary reinforcement theories of identificatory learning." *Journal of Abnormal and Social Psychology,* 67:527-534.

Bandura, Albert
1969 Principles of Behavior Modification. New York: Holt, Rinehart and Winston.

Barbour, Floyd B. (ed.)
1968 The Black Power Revolt. Boston: Porter Sargent

Baumrind, Diana
1966 "Effects of authoritative parental control on child behavior." Child Development, 37:888-907.

Bernard, Jessie
1966 Marriage and Family Among Negroes. Englewood Cliffs, New Jersey: Prentice-Hall Spectrum Books.

Blalock, Hubert M.
1964 Causal Inference in Nonexperimental Research. Chapel Hill, North Carolina: University of North Carolina Press.
1967 Toward A Theory of Minority Group Relations. New York: John Wiley & Sons.

Blalock, Hubert M., Jr.
1969 Theory Construction: From Verbal to Mathematical Formulations. Englewood Cliffs, New Jersey: Prentice-Hall, Inc.

Blau, Peter M. and Otis Dudley Duncan
1967 The American Occupational Structure. New York: John Wiley & Sons.

Blood, Robert O., Jr. and Robert L. Hamblin
1958 "The effects of the wife's employment in the family power structure." *Social Forces,* 26(May):347-352.

Bookstein, Fred L.
1970 "A new definition of 'path coefficient,'" mimeograph, Department of Sociology, Harvard University, Cambridge, Massachusetts 02138.

Bordua, David J.
1960 "Educational aspirations and parental stress on college." *Social Forces,* 38:262-269.

Boyle, Richard P.
1970 "Path analysis and ordinal data." *American Journal of Sociology,* 75(January): 461-480.

Bronfenbrenner, Urie
1958 "Socialization and social class through time and space." pp. 400-425 in E. E. Maccoby, T. M. Newcomb, and E. L. Hartley (eds.), Readings in Social Psychology. (3rd ed.) New York: Holt, Reinhart and Winston.

Brown, Claude
1965 Manchild In The Promised Land. New York: Signet Books.

Carmichael, Stokey and Charles V. Hamilton
1967 Black Power. New York: Random House Vintage Books.

Clark, Kenneth B. and Mamie P. Clark
1947 "Racial identification and preference in Negro children." pp. 169-178 in Theodore M. Newcomb and Eugene L. Hartley (eds.), Readings in Social Psychology. New York: Holt.
1965 Dark Ghetto. New York: Harper Torch Books.
1966 "The civil rights movement: Momentum and organization." pp. 595-625 in Parsons and Clark (1966).

Cleaver, Eldridge
1968 Soul On Ice. New York: Dell.

Cohen, Arthur R.
1959 "Some implications of self-esteem for social influence." pp. 102-118 in Carl I. Hovland and Irving L. Janis (eds.), *Personality and Persuasibility.* Volume II. New Haven: Yale University Press. Also pp. 383-390 in Gordon and Gergen (1968).

Coleman, James S.
1961 The Adolescent Society. New York: The Free Press.
1966 *et al.*
Equality of Educational Opportunity. Washington, D.C.: Office of Education, U.S. Department of Health, Education, and Welfare; Documents Catalog No. 5. 238: 38001.

Coles, Robert
1964 Children of Crisis. Boston: Little Brown & Co.

Combs, A. W. and D. Snygg
1948 Individual Behavior (revised ed.). New York: Harper and Brothers.

Coopersmith, Stanley
1967 The Antecedents of Self Esteem. San Francisco: W. H. Freeman.

Couch, Arthur S., *et al.*
1967 The DATA-TEXT System: A Computer Language for Social Sciences Research. Cambridge: Social Relations Computer Facility, Harvard University.

Crowne, Douglas P. and David Marlowe
1964 The Approval Motive: Studies in Evaluative Dependence. New York: Wiley.

David, Jay (ed.)
1968 Growing Up Black. New York: William Morrow and Company, Inc.

Davis, Allison and John Dollard
1940 Children of Bondage. New York: Harper Torch Book (1964).
1941 "American status systems and the socialization of the child." *American Sociological Review,* 6:345-354.
1941 Burleigh Gardner, and Mary Gardner
Deep South. Chicago: University of Chicago Press.
1947 and Robert J. Havighurst
Father of the Man. Boston: Houghton Mifflin

Deutsch, Martin
1964 "Social influence in Negro-white intelligence differences." *Journal of Social Issues,* 20:24-35.
1965 "The role of social class in language development and cognition." *American Journal of Orthopsychiatry,* 35(January):78-88.
1968 *et al.*
Social Class, Race, and Psychological Development. New York: Holt.

Dollard, John
1937 Caste and Class In A Southern Town. New York: Harper and Brothers.

Douvan, Elizabeth and Joseph Adelson
1966 The Adolescent Experience. New York: Wiley.

Drake, St. Clair and Horace Cayton
1945 Black Metropolis. New York: Harcourt, Brace & Co.
1965 "The social and economic status of the Negro in the United States." pp. 3-46 in Parsons and Clark (1966).

Duncan, Otis Dudley
1966 "Path analysis: sociological examples." *The American Journal of Sociology,* 72:1-16.
1968 "Socioeconomic Background and Occupational Achievement: Extensions of a Basic Model." Washington, D.C., Office of Education, Department of Health, Education, and Welfare; OEC-5-85-072.

Duncan, Otis Dudley, Archibald O. Haller, and Alejandro Portes
1968 "Peer influences on aspirations: a reinterpretation." *The American Journal of Sociology,* 74(September):119-137.

Duncan, Otis Dudley and Beverly Duncan
1969 "Family stability and occupational successes." *Social Problems* (Winter):273-285.

Dynes, Russell R., Alfred C. Clarke and Simon Dinitz
1956 "Level of occupational aspiration: some aspects of family experience as a variable." *American Sociological Review,* 21:212-215.

Eckland, Bruce K.
1965 "Academic ability, higher education and occupational mobility." *American Sociological Review,* 30:735-746.

Eisenstadt, S. N.
1956 From Generation to Generation. Glencoe, Illinois: The Free Press.

Elder, Glenn H., Jr.
1962a "Structural variations in the child rearing relationship." *Sociometry,* 25(September):241-262.
1962b Adolescent Achievement and Mobility Aspirations. Chapel Hill, North Carolina: University of North Carolina Press.
1963 "Parental power legitimation and its effect on the adolescent." *Sociometry,* 26(March):50-65.
1968 "Achievement motivation and intelligence in occupational mobility: a longitudinal analysis." *Sociometry,* 31(December):327-354.

Elkins, Stanley M.
1963 Slavery. New York: Grosset and Dunlap.

Ellison, Ralph
1947 Invisible Man. New York: Random House.

Empey, Lamar
1956 "Social class and occupational aspirations: a comparison of absolute and relative measurement." *American Sociological Review,* 21:703-709.

Erikson, Erik H.
1959 Identity and the Life Cycle. Monograph No. 1 of *Psychological Issues* contains "Growth and crises of the healthy personality," (1950) and "The problem of ego-identity," (1956).
1966 "The concept of identity in race relations." pp. 227-253 in Parsons and Clark (1966).

Fanon, Frantz
1967 Black Skin, White Masks. New York: Grove Press.

Fennessey, James
1968 "The general linear model: a new perspective on some familiar topics." *The American Journal of Sociology,* 74(July):1-27.

Ferman, Lois A., Joyce L. Kornbluth, and Alan Habler (eds.)
1965 Poverty in America. Ann Arbor: The University of Michigan Press.

Flanagan, John C., John T. Dailey, Marion F. Shaycoft, David B. Orr, and Isadore Goldberg
1962 A Survey and Follow-up Study of Educational Plans and Decisions in Relation to Aptitude Patterns: Studies of the American High School. Washington, D.C.: Office of Education, U.S. Department of Health, Education, and Welfare; CRP No. 226.

Flanagan, John C., *et al.*
1964 The American High School Student. Washington, D.C.: Office of Education, U.S. Department of Health, Education, and Welfare; CRP No. 635.

Flanagan, John C. and William W. Cooley
1966 Project Talent: One Year Follow-up Studies. Washington, D.C.: Office of Education, U.S. Department of Health, Education, and Welfare; CRP No. 2333.

Flavell, John H.
1963 The Developmental Psychology of Jean Piaget. Princeton, New Jersey: D. Van Nostrand.

Frazier, E. Franklin
1937 "The impact of urban civilization upon Negro family life." *American Sociological Review,* 2:609-618.
1939 The Negro Family in the United States. Revised and abridged edition published in 1948 by the Dryden Press and issued as University of Chicago Phoenix paperback (1966).
1957 Black Bourgeoisie. New York: The Free Press.

Fromm, Erich
1939 "Selfishness and self-love." *Psychiatry,* 2:507-523; reprinted in somewhat condensed form in Gordon and Gergen (1968:327-337).

Ginzberg, Eli and John L. Herma
1964 Talent and Performance. New York: Columbia University Press.

Glazer, Nathan and Daniel P. Moynihan
1963 Beyond the Melting Pot. Cambridge, Massachusetts: The M.I.T. Press and Harvard University Press.

Goffman, Erving
1955 "On face work: an analysis of the ritual elements in social interaction." *Psychiatry,* 18:213-231; also reprinted in Gordon and Gergen (1968:309-325).
1959 The Presentation of Self in Everyday Life. Garden City, New Jersey: Doubleday Anchor Books.

Goldstein, Bernard
1967 Low Income Youth in Urban Areas. New York: Holt, Rinehart and Winston.

Goode, William J.
1965 The Family. Englewood Cliffs, New Jersey: Prentice-Hall.

Goodman, Mary Ellen
1952 Race Awareness In Young Children. Reading, Massachusetts: Addison Wesley.

Gordon, Chad
1963 Self-Conception and Social Achievement. Doctoral dissertation, U.C.L.A., Ann Arbor: University Microfilms.
1966 "Self-conceptions: configurations of content." Chapter 11 in Gordon and Gergen (1968).
1967 and Paul D. Shea
"Self-conceptions and family structures of disadvantaged youth." Presented at the 1967 meetings of the American Sociological Association, San Francisco
1968a "Systemic senses of self." *Sociological Inquiry,* 38(Spring):161-177.
1968b "Self-conceptions methodologies." *Journal of Nervous and Mental Disease,* 148(April, 1969):328-364.
1968c "On the sense of personal autonomy." Presented at the Eastern Sociological Society meetings, April 1968. Copies available from the author.
1968 and Kenneth J. Gergen (eds.)
The Self in Social Interaction: Volume I, Classic and Contemporary Perspectives. New York: John Wiley and Company.
1969 "Socialization across the life-cycle: a stage developmental model." Social Relations Department, Harvard University; multilith.

Green, Arnold W.
1946 "The middle-class male child and neurosis." *American Sociological Review,* 11(February):31-41.

Grier, William H. and Price M. Cobbs
1968 Black Rage. New York: Basic Books.

Haley, Alex and Malcolm X
1964 The Autobiography of Malcolm X. New York: The Grove Press.

Harrington, Michael
1963 The Other America. New York: Macmillan.

Havighurst, Robert J. and Hilda Taba
1949 Adolescent Character and Personality. New York: Wiley.
1962 Growing Up In River City. New York: Wiley.

Heise, David R.
1969 "Problems in path analysis and causal inference." pp. 38-73 in Edgar F. Borgatta (ed.), Sociological Methodology, 1969. San Francisco: Jossey-Bass, 1969.

Herzog, Elizabeth
1966 "Is there a breakdown of the Negro family?" pp. 344-354 in Rainwater and Yancey (1967).

Hollingshead, August B.
1949 Elmtown's Youth. New York: Wiley.

Horney, Karen
1945 The Neurotic Personality of Our Time. New York: W. W. Norton and Company.

Inkeles, Alex
1968 "Society, social structure and child socialization." pp. 73-129 in John A. Clausen (ed.), Socialization and Society. Boston: Little Brown and Company.

Jensen, Arthur R.
1968a "Social class and verbal learning." pp. 115-174 in Deutsch, et al. (1968).
1968b "How much can we boost I.Q. and scholastic achievement?" pp. 1-123 in Environment, Heredity, and Intelligence, Reprint Series No. 2, Harvard Educational Review, 1969.

Kagan, Jerome and Howard A. Moss
1962 Birth to Maturity. New York: Wiley.

Kagan, Jerome
1964 "Acquisition and significance of sex-typing and sex role identity." pp. 137-168 in Martin L. Hoffman and Lois W. Hoffman (eds.), Review of Child Development Research, Vol. I, New York: Russell Sage Foundation, 1964.

Kahl, Joseph
1953 "Educational and occupational aspirations of 'common man' boys." *Harvard Educational Review,* 23:186-203.

Kardiner, Abram and Lionel Ovesey
1951 The Mark of Oppression. New York: World Publishing Co.

Keil, Charles
1966 Urban Blues. Chicago: The University of Chicago Press.

Killian, Lewis
1968 The Impossible Revolution?: Black Power and the American Dream. New York: Random House.

Knupfer, Genevieve
1947 "Portrait of the underdog." *Public Opinion Quarterly,* 11:103-114.

Kochman, Thomas
1969 " 'Rapping' in the black ghetto." *Trans-action,* 6(February):26-34.

Kozol, Jonathan
1967 Death at an Early Age. Boston: Houghton Mifflin Co.

Land, Kenneth C.
1969 "Principles of path analysis." in Edgar F. Borgatta (ed.), Sociological Methodology, 1969. San Francisco: Jossey-Bass, 1969.

Lecky, Prescott
1945 Self consistency: A Theory of Personality. Long Island, New York: The Island Press.

Lewin, Kurt *et al.*
1944 "Level of aspiration." pp. 333-378 in J. McV. Hunt (ed.), Personality and the Behavior Disorders, Volume I, New York: The Ronald Press.
1948 Resolving Social Conflicts. New York: Harper and Brothers.

Lewis, Oscar
1965 La Vida. New York: Random House.

Lidz, Theodore
1968 The Person: His Development Throughout the Life Cycle. New York: Basic Books, Inc.

Liebow, Elliot
1966 Tally's Corner. Boston: Little, Brown and Company.

Lipset, Seymour M. and Hans L. Zetterberg
1956 "A theory of social mobility." Transactions of the Third World Congress of Sociology, 2:155-177.

Lott, Albert J. and Bernice E. Lott
1962 "Negro and white children's plans for their futures." pp. 347-361 in Joan I. Roberts (ed.), School Children in the Urban Slum (1967). New York: The Free Press.

Lynn, David B.
1966 "The process of learning parental and sex-role identification." *Journal of Marriage and the Family,* 28:466-470.

Maccoby, Eleanor E.
1958 "Effects upon children of their mothers' outside employment." pp. 150-172 of her work in The Lives of Married Women. New York: Columbia University Press.

McCall, George J., and J. L. Simmons
1966 Identities and Interactions. New York: The Free Press.

Merton, Robert K.
1957 "Social structure and anomie." pp. 131-160 in his Social Theory and Social Structure (revised edition) Glencoe, Illinois: The Free Press.

Mischel, W.
1958 "Preference for delayed reinforcement: an experimental study of cultural observation." *Journal of Abnormal and Social Psychology,* 56:57-61.

Moynihan, Daniel P.
1965 "The Negro family: the case for national action." ("The Moynihan Report"). Office of Policy, Planning and Research, U.S. Department of Labor; most readily available in Rainwater and Yancey (1967): 44-124. (Page citations refer to the Rainwater and Yancey volume.)
1966 "Employment, income, and the ordeal of the Negro family." pp. 134-159 in Parsons and Clark (eds.), 1966.

National Advisory Commission on Civil Disorders
1968 Report. Also called "The Riot Commission Report" or "The Kerner Commission Report." New York: Bantam Books and the New York Times Company.

Osipow, Samuel H.
1968 Theories of Career Development. New York: Appleton-Century-Crofts.

Parsons, Talcott and Robert F .Bales
1955 Family, Socialization and Interaction Process. Glencoe, Illinois: The Free Press.
1966 and Kenneth B. Clark (eds.)
The Negro American. New York: Houghton Mifflin Beacon paperback edition of *Daedalus* 1965 (Fall) and 1966 (Winter) issues.

Pavenstedt, Eleanor
1965 "A comparison of the child-rearing practices of upper-lower and very low-lower-class families." *American Journal of Orthopsychiatry,* 35:89-98.
1967 *et al.* (eds.)
The Drifters: Children of Disorganized Lower-Class Families. Boston: Little, Brown and Co.

Pepitone, Albert
1968 "An experimental analysis of self-dynamics." pp. 347-354 in Gordon and Gergen (1968).

Pettigrew, Thomas F.
1964 A Profile of the Negro American. Princeton, New Jersey: D. Van Nostrand.
1965 "Complexity and change in American racial patterns: a social psychological view." pp. 325-359 in Parsons and Clark (1966).
1968 "Racially separate or together?" Society for the Psychological Study of Social Issues presidential address, printed in *Journal of Social Issues,* 25(January):43-69.

Podell, Lawrence
1969 Families on Welfare in New York City. New York: The Center for the Study of Urban Problems, City University of New York.

Proshansky, Harold and Peggy Newton
1968 "The nature and meaning of Negro self-identity." pp. 178-218 in Martin Deutsch *et al.* (1968).

Rainwater, Lee
1966 "Crucible of identity: the Negro lower-class family." pp. 160-204 in Parsons and Clark, eds., (1966).
1967 and William L. Yancey (eds.)
The Moynihan Report and the Politics of Controversy. Cambridge, Massachusetts: The M.I.T. Press.

Rogers, Carl R.
1950 "The significance of the self-regarding attitudes and perceptions." pp. 374-382 in Martin L. Reymert (ed.), Feeling and Emotion. New York: McGraw-Hill. Also reprinted in Gordon and Gergen (1968):435-441.

Rohrer, John H. and Munro S. Edmonson (eds.)
1960 The Eighth Generation Grows Up. New York: Harper and Row.

Rosen, Bernard C.
1956 "The achievement syndrome: a psychocultural dimension of social stratification." *American Sociological Review,* 21:203-211.
1959 "Race, ethnicity, and the achievement syndrome." *American Sociological Review,* 24:47-60.
1959 and Roy D'Andrade
"The psychological origins of achievement motivation." *Sociometry,* 22(September): 185-218.
1961 "Family structure and achievement motivation." *American Sociological Review,* 26:574-585.
1969 Harry J. Crockett, and Clyde Z. Nunn (eds.)
Achievement in American Society. Cambridge, Massachusetts: Schenkman Publishing Company.

Rosen, Lawrence
1969 "Matriarchy and lower-class Negro male delinquency." *Social Problems,* 17 (Fall):175-189.

Rosenberg, Morris
1957 Occupations and Values. Glencoe, Illinois: The Free Press.
1963 "Parental interest and children's self-conceptions." *Sociometry,* 26(March): 35-49.
1965 Society and the Adolescent Self-Image. Princeton, New Jersey: Princeton University Press.
1967 "Psychological selectivity in self-esteem formation." pp. 26-50 in Carolyn W. Sherif and Muzafer Sherif (eds.), Attitude, Ego-Involvement and Change. New York: Wiley; also reprinted in Gordon and Gergen (1968:339-346).

Rosenthal, Robert and Leonore Jacobson
1968 Pygmalion In the Classroom: Teacher Expectation and Pupils' Intellectual Development. New York: Holt, Rinehart, and Winston.

Rotter, Julian B.
1966 "Generalized expectancies for internal versus external control of reinforcement." *Psychological Monographs,* 80, No. 1:1-28.

Schutz, Alfred
1932 The Phenomenology of the Social World. Translated by George Walsh and Frederick Lehnert. Evanston, Illinois: Northwestern University Press (1967).

Sears, Pauline S. and Vivian S. Sherman
1964 In Pursuit of Self-Esteem. Belmont, California: Wadsworth Publishing Company.

Sears, R. R., M. H. Pintler and P. S. Sears
1946 "Effect of father separation on preschool children's doll play aggression." *Child Development,* 17:219-243.

Seeman, Melvin
1959 "On the meaning of alientation." *American Sociological Review,* 24:783-791.

Sewell, William H., Archie O. Haller, and Murray A. Strauss
1957 "Social status and educational and occupational aspiration." *American Sociological Review,* 22:67-73.
1967 and Vimal P. Shah
"Socioeconomic status, intelligence, and the attainment of higher education." *Sociology of Education,* 40:1-23.

Sewell, William H., Archie O. Haller, and Murray A Strauss (continued)
1968 and Vimal P. Shah
"Parents' education and children's educational aspirations and achievements." *American Sociological Review,* 33:191-209.

Sewell, William H., Archibald O. Haller, and Alejandro Portes
1969 "The educational and early occupational attainment process." *American Sociological Review,* 34(February):82-92.

Sheppard, Harold L. and Herbert E. Striner
1966 "Family structure and employment problems." pp. 354-368 in Rainwater and Yancey (1967).

Shibutani, Tamotsu
1961 Society and Personality. Englewood Cliffs, New Jersey: Prentice-Hall.

Silberman, Charles
1964 Crisis in Black and White. New York: Random House Vintage Books.

Simpson, George E. and J. Milton Yinger
1965 Racial and Cultural Minorities (2nd ed.). New York: Harper and Row.

Slocum, Walter L.
1966 Occupational Careers: A Sociological Perspective. Chicago: Aldine Publishing Company.

Smith, M. Brewster
1968 "Competence and socialization." pp. 271-320 in John A. Clausen (ed.), Socialization and Society. Boston: Little, Brown and Company.

Somers, Robert H.
1962 "A new asymmetric measure of association for ordinal variables." *American Sociological Review,* 27:799-811.

Sorokin, Pitirim A.
1927 Social and Cultural Mobility. Glencoe, Illinois: The Free Press (1959), reprinting of Social Mobility (1927).

Stephenson, Richard M.
1957 "Mobility orientation and stratification for 1,000 ninth graders." *American Sociological Review,* 22:204-212.

Stonequist, Everett V.
1937 The Marginal Man. New York: Scribner.

Toby, Jackson
1957 "Orientation to education as a factor in the school maladjustment of lower-class children." *Social Forces,* 35:259-266.

Turner, Ralph H.
1960 "Sponsored and contest mobility and the school system." *American Sociological Review,* 25:855-867.
1964 The Social Context of Ambition. San Francisco: Chandler Publishing Company.
1966 "The self-conception in social interaction." Chapter 9 in Gordon and Gergen (1968).

U.S. Civil Rights Commission
1967 Racial Isolation in the Public Schools. Washington, D.C.: U.S. Government Printing Office.

Veblen, Thorstein
1899 The Theory of the Leisure Class. New York: The Macmillan Co.

Warner, W. Lloyd and Leo Srole
1945 The Social Systems of American Ethnic Groups. New Haven, Connecticut: Yale University Press.

Whiteman, Martin and Martin Deutsch
1968 "Social disadvantage as related to intellective and language development." pp. 86-114 in Deutsch, et al. (1968).

Whiting, John and Roger Burton
1961 "The absent father and cross-sex identity." *Merrill-Palmer Quarterly*, 7:85-95.

Wright, Richard
1937 Black Boy. New York: Signet Books.

Wylie, Ruth
1961 The Self-Concept. Lincoln, Nebraska: University of Nebraska Press.

Yarrow, L. J.
1964 "Separation from adults during early childhood." pp. 89-136 in M. L. Hoffman and L. U. Hoffman (eds.), Review of Child Development Research, Vol. I. New York: Russell Sage Foundation.